ORGANICS
HappyFAMILY®
organic superfoods COOKBOOK
FOR BABY&TODDLER

by SHAZI VISRAM
FOUNDER & CHIEF MOM OF HAPPY FAMILY

with CRICKET AZIMA
FOUNDER & BIG CHEESE OF THE CREATIVE KITCHEN

photography by TARA DONNE

characters by HAPPY FAMILY

weldon**owen**

CONTENTS

A HAPPY, HEALTHY START

⇥1⇤ SIMPLE BABY PUREES

4+ months, starting solids

⇥2⇤ BABY MEALS

6+ months, flavorful combos

THE HAPPY FAMILY STORY

Almost thirteen years ago, I had this crazy idea to change the world for the better by making organic baby food. Happy Family—first called Happy Baby—started with an aha moment talking to a mommy friend and then became an all-consuming business in my tiny galley kitchen in Brooklyn in 2003, with an official launch on Mother's Day 2006. Happy Family has a social mission at its core: to change the way children are fed in our country in order to improve their health and happiness. My constantly expanding and evolving line of premade organic, sustainable meals and snacks for babies and toddlers is the proud accomplishment of that mission.

So, why give away our recipes in a cookbook? Although I believe that the products Happy Family offers are the best you can buy (made by moms and dads who care about the safety and nutrition of children at every stage), the truth is you really can't beat homemade.

I believe it is every parent's aspiration to give the love, care, and freshness of homemade food to their kids. But there have been times when my son ate only our premade products because I had no time to catch a breath. Trust me—I get it that we all go through those phases. And, while Happy Family products are truly something you can feel good about giving your baby, I want to support your cooking delicious and nutritious recipes when you find the time to cook because really good things happen the more we connect with and know about our food.

When I first started this journey, I didn't yet have a baby of my own. But I knew that babies have vulnerable and rapidly developing bodies that need nutritious food to support their best start in life—and that Happy Family could make a difference by giving babies real, pure foods from their first bite. Babies develop tastes and preferences at a very early age that can last a lifetime, so why not provide them with the freshest and cleanest food from the very beginning? I now have a six-year-old rascal boy, Zane, and a baby girl on the way, so more than ever I realize how the health and quality of our food is so vital for the health and quality of our lives.

This cookbook celebrates ten years of Happy Family and is all about sharing the wealth of knowledge from moms to moms—real information to make life easier and better for your baby's wellness. I partnered with chef and fellow mom Cricket Azima to create recipes that reflect our Enlightened Nutrition Philosophy. Tips are sprinkled throughout by our team of caring moms who have been around the block (a few times) and have learned a lot about health, nutrition, and food that they want to share with you.

So let's all take time to enjoy the happy moments and eat yummy bites along the way!

Shazi

OUR ENLIGHTENED NUTRITION PHILOSOPHY

What your baby eats and experiences during the first 1,000 days—from the moment of conception to baby's second birthday—has lifelong consequences for health. Children develop their taste preferences starting in the womb, so exposing your children from an early age to foods made with a wide variety of fruits and vegetables helps them develop a taste for these foods and lays the foundation for healthy eating habits. Later on, this foundation might mean the difference between reaching for an apple over a bag of chips.

Enlightened Nutrition is all about using nature's best ingredients to amplify the nutritional content in our recipes based on your child's age-and-stage needs. In this book, we support your efforts to give your precious little one the best start in life by sharing recipes that showcase these nutrient-rich and delicious ingredients in ways that your baby or toddler will enjoy.

You probably noticed that we've called this an organic cookbook. Why is that? We believe that whole organic foods are best for babies. Organic fruits, vegetables, and grains are grown without pesticides, genetically modified organisms (GMOs), or most synthetic fertilizers. Organic meats are from animals raised without antibiotics and growth hormones. Studies have shown that when children eat organic foods, they ingest far fewer pesticide residues than those who eat only conventional foods—so it's about protecting our little ones.[1]

Organic farming can be more labor-intensive than modern conventional farming, which usually means higher prices at the grocery store. But despite the increased cost, many people believe that the benefits of eating organic food more than justify the extra expense, especially when it comes to produce on the "Dirty Dozen" list—that is, those fruits and vegetables with the most toxic, persistent pesticides remaining on them after harvest. The Dirty Dozen often includes many year-round favorites, such as apples, celery, cherries, cherry tomatoes, cucumbers, grapes, nectarines, peaches, spinach, strawberries, sweet bell peppers, and tomatoes. The good news is that many people choose to trim their grocery bill by buying conventionally grown (not organic) fruits and vegetables from the "Clean Fifteen" list—those foods with the lowest amount of pesticide residue. Every year, the Environmental Working Group publishes an updated list on its website.

SUPERFOODS

Superfoods are nutrient powerhouses. They are foods that pack a lot of benefit into a small package, so they are a great way to boost your baby's nutrition. You'll see many of these tasty ingredients featured in recipes in this book.

AMARANTH This ancient seed and staple grain contains more protein than most grains, and it's gluten-free.

BLUEBERRIES The antioxidants and flavonoids in blueberries pack a large nutrition punch. They are linked to preventing heart disease and cancer in adults.

CHIA SEEDS These tiny seeds contain more omega-3 fatty acids than some fish oils! They're also a good source of fiber and protein.

KALE This dark green leafy vegetable is in the same cruciferous family as broccoli and cauliflower. Its superb antioxidant and anti-inflammatory nutrients are known to have a role in preventing cancer in adults.

KEFIR & YOGURT Kefir is a fermented yogurt-type drink. Like yogurt, kefir is a source of live active probiotic cultures that support immune function and digestive health.

POMEGRANATE Tart and delicious, the seeds of the pomegranate contain more antioxidant power than most other fruits.

QUINOA This gluten-free seed, which many think of as a grain, is rich in protein, fiber, and iron. It was so sacred to the ancient Incas that they called it the "mother grain."

SPINACH Always at the top of nutrient-rich food lists, spinach contains high concentrations of antioxidant nutrients, including vitamin A, vitamin C, vitamin E, and folate.

WILD SALMON Easy to prepare and mild in flavor, wild salmon is a tremendous source of DHA, which is an omega-3 fatty acid that's important for baby's brain development. Unlike some other types of fish, salmon is low in the contaminant mercury.

[1] Hunter, D et al. "Evaluation of the micronutrient composition of plant foods produced by organic and conventional agricultural methods," *Crit Rev Food Sci Nutr.* 51, no. 6 (2011): 571-82.

KEY NUTRIENTS FOR YOUR BABY & TODDLER

Making healthy homemade baby food is one of the best things you can do for your baby, placing the mix of nutrients and flavors that baby enjoys firmly in your hands.

As a parent, you want to know what is in each recipe you're cooking for your little one and why the ingredients are important. That's why we've shared the key nutrient info for each meal and snack recipe so you can rest assured that your baby is eating well. Here's a quick rundown of these nutrients, where they are found, and why they are important.

NUTRIENT	WHERE IT'S FOUND	WHY IT'S IMPORTANT
CALCIUM	*Milk, yogurt, cheese, dark green vegetables (such as collards), tofu, chia seeds*	Supports strong bones and teeth
CHOLINE	*Eggs, meat, breast milk, fortified foods*	Supports brain development
FIBER	*Whole grains (including whole-grain cereals and pastas), brown rice, fruits, vegetables, beans*	Helps with bowel regularity (prevents constipation)
IRON	*Beef, chicken, tofu, beans, lentils, dark green vegetables (such as spinach and broccoli), fortified breakfast cereals, dried fruit, whole grains*	Helps the blood carry oxygen to cells and muscles
OMEGA-3 FATTY ACIDS	*Cold-water fish (like salmon), algae, walnuts, canola oil, fortified foods*	Supports brain and eye health
PREBIOTICS	*Chicories, jicama, fortified foods*	Provides the energy source for probiotics
PROBIOTICS	*Fermented foods (such as yogurt, kefir, and sauerkraut), breast milk*	"Friendly bacteria" that support immune function and digestive health
PROTEIN	*Beef, chicken, fish, turkey, tofu, beans, lentils, quinoa, eggs, milk, yogurt, cheese, nuts, nut butters*	Supports growth and development
VITAMIN A	*Dark green vegetables (such as spinach and kale), orange and yellow fruits and vegetables (such as carrots, cantaloupe, and squash)*	Supports vision and a strong immune system
VITAMIN B, INCLUDING FOLIC ACID, B6, AND B12	*Folic acid (folate): beans, leafy green vegetables, asparagus, oranges, mangoes, whole grains. B6: poultry, fish, beans. B12: meats, fish, dairy, eggs*	Converts fats, proteins, and carbohydrates into energy the body can use
VITAMIN C	*Citrus, broccoli, potatoes, bell peppers, strawberries*	Helps with iron absorption
VITAMIN D	*Eggs, fortified dairy products, fortified foods*	Supports bone health

FEEDING YOUR BABY

READY TO EAT?

The American Academy of Pediatrics (AAP) recommends introducing solid foods around six months of age. Before this age, breast milk is best, as it provides all the nutrition your baby requires. By six months, most breast-fed babies need additional iron, and all babies benefit from exposure to more flavors, textures, and eating skills.

But that's not to say that all babies follow the same timetable, so be sure to observe your baby to determine when she's ready to begin her solid food adventures.

Baby's probably ready to eat solid foods when:

- She no longer has the reflex that causes her to push out with her tongue; instead, she can take food from a spoon and swallow.
- She can sit with support.
- She holds her head straight up when sitting, and she can turn her head toward or away from food.
- She appears interested in food when others are eating.
- She opens her mouth when offered a spoonful of food.

INTRODUCING YOUR BABY TO NEW FOODS

These days, there are few rules about when to introduce specific foods. It's all about making sure you are giving baby the right texture for her stage of development—a texture she can swallow safely. Use this guide for some ideas.

AGE & STAGE	GRAINS/CEREALS	FRUITS	VEGETABLES	PROTEIN FOODS
4–6 MONTHS *Start with pureed, strained, easy-to-swallow foods*	Amaranth Barley (cereal or pureed) Oatmeal Quinoa Rice (cereal or pureed)	Pureed or well-mashed: Apples Apricots Bananas Peaches Pears Plums	Pureed or well-mashed: Avocado Green beans Peas Summer squash Sweet Potatoes Winter squash	Pureed and strained meats
7–9 MONTHS *Add more texture, progressing to coarsely mashed or finely chopped foods*	Bits of soft bread Lumpier oatmeal, other hot cereal, or dry O-type cereal Cooked pasta	Coarsely mashed: Mango Papaya Pineapple	Coarsely mashed: Asparagus Beets Broccoli Cauliflower Cucumber Spinach	Egg yolk Mashed beans Mashed lentils Mashed or finely ground beef, chicken, lamb, pork, or turkey Yogurt (plain whole-milk)
8–12 MONTHS *When ready, add more finger foods*	Biscuits Dry cereal Puffs Cooked pasta	Small pieces of soft peeled fruit Pineapple	Small pieces of cooked or soft peeled vegetables	Cottage cheese and other mild cheeses Fish Small pieces of cooked beans and meats Tofu

BABY SERVING SIZES

This chart shows daily solid-food intake for babies up to one year old, but these are suggestions—not rules. Every baby is a bit different and may eat more or less. Typically, babies who are just starting solid foods will start with about 1 tablespoon at a time of any given food and work up to about 4 tablespoons (¼ cup) of each food on their plate when they are twelve months old. Breast milk or formula feedings (not shown here) continue to provide the bulk of baby's nutrients up to age one year. (Note: All serving sizes are aligned with recommendations from the AAP.)

	4-6 MONTHS	6-8 MONTHS	8-10 MONTHS	10-12 MONTHS
BREAKFAST	1–2 Tbsp cereal 1–2 Tbsp fruit and/or veg	2–4 Tbsp cereal 2–4 Tbsp fruit and/or veg	4–6 Tbsp cereal 2–4 Tbsp fruit and/or veg	4–6 Tbsp cereal 2–4 Tbsp fruit and/or veg
LUNCH	n/a	1 serving grain* 2–4 Tbsp fruit and/or veg	2–4 Tbsp protein 2–4 Tbsp fruit and/or veg 1 serving grain*	2–4 Tbsp protein 3–4 Tbsp fruit and/or veg 1 serving grain*
DINNER	1–2 Tbsp cereal 1–2 Tbsp fruit	1–3 Tbsp protein 2–4 Tbsp fruit and/or veg 1 serving grain*	2–4 Tbsp protein 2–4 Tbsp fruit and/or veg 1 serving grain*	2–4 Tbsp protein 3–4 Tbsp fruit and/or veg
SNACKS	n/a	½ serving dairy**	1 serving grain* or dairy** 2–4 Tbsp fruit and/or veg	3–4 Tbsp fruit and/or veg 1 serving grain* ½ serving dairy**

*1 serving grain = ½ cup cereal, ½ cup cooked grain, ½ slice bread, or 2 crackers
**1 serving dairy = ½ cup yogurt or 1 ounce cheese

KEEPING BABY HEALTHY

As with any choice you make for your child, it's always best to be well informed and knowledgeable regarding your options and best practices. Follow these food safety tips to keep your baby's food fresh and free of contaminants:

- Before preparing food, always wash your hands and make sure your tools and work surface are clean.

- Rinse all fresh fruits and vegetables thoroughly with fresh, running water prior to use, even if you're removing the skin.

- If you're cooking raw meat, poultry, or fish, be sure to avoid cross-contamination with other foods: wash your hands immediately after handling these raw ingredients, and use clean utensils and a clean work surface for preparing other items.

- Thaw meat in the refrigerator, not at room temperature.

- Always cook meat, poultry, and fish until they reach the proper internal temperature. Use a meat thermometer to measure these doneness temperatures:
    Chicken and turkey: 165°F
    Beef, lamb, and pork: 160°F
    Fish: 145°F

SHAZI'S TIP

Moms often ask us which cookware is the safest to use, and I like to recommend the tried-and-true types: cast iron is my top choice, followed by stainless steel and ceramic cookware. I also use glass for baking.

FOODS TO AVOID OR DELAY

Though the AAP does not recommend delaying the introduction of common allergens for most babies, one food remains on the no-no list for babies under one year old: honey. Honey may contain spores of *Clostridium botulinum*, which can cause botulism. Adults' immune systems can handle a small amount of these spores, but babies under one year are susceptible to a life-threatening reaction to the toxins the bacteria produce.

Other foods are choking hazards for babies and should be delayed until your child is two to three years old. Use caution when giving your baby these riskier foods, and ensure she is fully chewing them:

- Nuts and seeds

- Popcorn

- Sticky foods, such as chewing gum, jelly candies, and marshmallows

- Raisins

- Whole grapes

- Uncut hot dogs or sausage links

- Hard candy

- Too-large chunks of meat or other tough foods

- Raw carrots

FOOD ALLERGIES: WHAT TO LOOK FOR

The majority of babies will never develop a single food allergy. But if your baby has a sibling or parent with a food allergy or allergic condition, your pediatrician may recommend delaying the introduction of certain foods just in case. The most common food allergens are wheat, soy, milk, eggs, fish, shellfish, tree nuts, and peanuts.

We label our recipes at the top of each page to show which are dairy-free, egg-free, gluten-free, nut-free, and vegetarian. We also suggest some "switch it up" tips for recipes that include some common allergens (for example, dairy or wheat) so all babies can enjoy these delicious meals.

As you introduce new foods, be sure to observe how baby tolerates them so that you can identify any potential issues. Introduce foods one at a time, waiting three or four days before starting another new food. Don't be concerned if the color and texture of your baby's stool changes during this time—these changes are normal and usually do not indicate a problem.

Signs of allergy or intolerance include a new skin rash, vomiting or diarrhea, or blood in the stool. If you think baby is allergic to a food, eliminate it from the diet and see if the symptoms disappear. Tell your pediatrician about any new symptoms you observe or if you suspect a food allergy.

GLUTEN-FREE COOKING

Gluten is a protein found in wheat that helps give dough an elastic and chewy texture and allows it to rise in the oven. For some children, gluten proteins can be harder to digest and can cause inflammation, so we like to limit gluten during baby's first year as the digestive system is strengthening. If you have a family history of celiac disease or gluten intolerance and choose to limit it, there are many tasty gluten-free grains and starches available. Rice, especially brown rice, is a gluten-free mainstay. There's also amaranth, buckwheat (which isn't actually a wheat), millet, quinoa, and sorghum. If you are avoiding gluten, the important thing is to not just rely on processed packaged "gluten-free" foods. It's easy to cook whole grains and whole foods without gluten—as you'll discover in many of the yummy recipes in this book.

SALT & OTHER FLAVOR-ENHANCERS

Babies need very little sodium and have not yet developed any preference for a salty taste, but that doesn't mean the food you serve should be bland. Feel free to add a little salt when cooking to enhance the flavor of food. Or add other flavor-enhancing ingredients, such as fresh herbs and spices, unsalted butter or olive oil, balsamic or apple cider vinegar, lemon or lime juice, or alliums like garlic, onion, shallots, scallions, and leeks.

SUGAR SUBSTITUTIONS

It's true that babies (and toddlers, of course) tend to prefer sweeter tastes, but they don't need added sugar—they're sweet enough! If you want to lend a sweet and appealing flavor to foods and cut the bitterness of certain ingredients without sprinkling on the sugar, here are some ideas:

SWEET VEGETABLES: *beets, carrots, sweet potatoes. Boil or roast and then puree to add to soups, baked goods, casseroles, and sauces. Or, shred and mix in with other ingredients in ground-meat dishes, casseroles, and even muffins and pancakes.*

FRUITS: *apples, bananas, fruit purees, pears. These are your go-to natural sweets. Pair with plain yogurt, put in baked goods, and cook with meats.*

SWEET SPICES: *cinnamon, vanilla powder. A little of these spices goes a long way in your baked goods.*

FEEDING A TODDLER

During the toddler stage, your baby will continue to discover new foods. At times, these discoveries will be met with joy, and at other times, resistance. If you find that your toddler is becoming picky, don't worry. Read on for some perspective and helpful tips. The recipes in this book will help you tuck powerful nutrition into a tasty (and maybe even fun) toddler-friendly package.

FACTS ABOUT TODDLERS & PICKY EATING

Toddlers and preschoolers can indeed be picky when it comes to food. It's common for young children to refuse to eat new foods or even foods that they once enjoyed. Some are very particular about which plate they use at mealtime. Others dissolve into a weepy mess if their foods touch each other on the plate. It can be frustrating for you as a parent, especially if you believe your child isn't eating enough. It may help to understand what's going on behind the scenes at this age:

Toddlers may not feel very hungry.
Their growth significantly slows down in the second and third years. Consider this: your baby's weight tripled in the first year, but in the second, there might be a gain of only about five pounds.

The toddler years are when kids are becoming more independent.
Does "I do it myself!" sound familiar? Some picky eating is just the child exerting a newfound independence.

Toddlers tend to fear new things.
Foods that look unfamiliar can be scary to them, which is one reason toddlers like to eat the same foods over and over.

Teething can make a toddler's mouth feel sore.
The promise of pain, even when slight, can make food seem quite unappealing.

Most toddlers are easily distracted.
Toddlers simply may not have the attention span to sit through a long meal.

Toddlers like to test limits.
They want to see what happens if they refuse to eat their meal or if they throw their food on the floor.

INSTILLING HEALTHY EATING HABITS

Just because it's normal for toddlers to be picky doesn't mean you should give up and give in to their every whim. Now more than ever, it's important to help shape their healthy eating habits. Here are some strategies:

Allow your child to decide how much food to eat. Offer foods that are healthful and tasty, then don't punish or scold a child who chooses not to eat. Avoid bribes: you're trying to teach your child to enjoy healthy foods, not to perform for a reward, such as "If you finish your vegetables, you can ride your tricycle after dinner!"

Have realistic expectations. For example, toddlers can't sit still for very long, so don't call your child to the table until his meal is at his place and ready to go.

Let your toddler have a role in meal planning without surrendering entirely to his whim. For example, let him pick the pasta shape or ask if he would like either broccoli or green beans with dinner.

Have a routine. Try to serve your toddler's three meals and two snacks at the table and at around the same time every day. When tots know what to expect, they feel more secure.

Indulge their love for fun! Arrange foods on the plate in the shape of a smiley face. Or, cut foods into different shapes—for example, use cookie cutters to stamp out fun-shaped sandwiches.

PORTION SIZES FOR TODDLERS

The portion sizes shown here are a guide from the AAP, not a strict rule. Your toddler's basic nutrition needs will be met if she's eating the minimum number of servings shown here. For grains, an upper limit is given to help you avoid overfeeding these toddler favorites.

FOOD GROUP	SERVINGS PER DAY	PORTION SIZE
DAIRY	2 or 3 servings	½ cup whole milk ½ oz cheese ⅓ cup whole-milk yogurt
FRUIT	2 or 3 servings	¼–⅓ cup cooked or chopped fruit ½ piece fresh fruit ¼ cup 100% fruit juice
GRAINS	6–11 servings	⅓ cup cooked grains ⅓ cup dry cereal ½ slice bread 2 or 3 crackers
PROTEIN	2 servings	1 oz meat, fish, chicken, turkey, or tofu ¼ cup beans ½ egg
VEGETABLES	2 or 3 servings	¼ cup cooked or raw chopped veggies

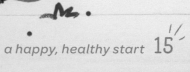

BEST METHODS FOR STORAGE

REFRIGERATING BABY'S FOOD

The recipes in this book supply much more than a baby can consume in a single sitting. Luckily, all can be stored in an airtight container in the refrigerator to be ready for future feedings.

For best refrigerator storage practices, make sure the food you prepared has cooled completely, then transfer to an airtight container. Leftovers from your cooking pan should be refrigerated within an hour (especially if you are working with any perishable food). You can leave meals in the fridge for two to three days.

Reheat baby's food in individual portion sizes, and discard any that is reheated and not consumed.

Handle leftovers safely: If the spoon that has been in your child's mouth has also been in the food container, discard the leftovers, as bacteria from the mouth can grow in the food (consider scooping food into a clean bowl for serving to avoid contamination of a full container of food). Similarly, do not refrigerate the leftovers from your baby's plate since that food has been in contact with baby's saliva and could have bacteria in it that will multiply if refrigerated.

FREEZING BABY'S FOOD

Many parents find it helpful to have a go-to supply of foods in the freezer for days when there is no time to cook. Freeze leftovers or make a double batch and use one and freeze one. Here are some tips for using your freezer stash[1]:

- **Freeze baby food in small portions so it's easy to thaw just the amount that you need.** Spoon purees into the cups of a muffin tin or ice cube tray and cover with plastic wrap; once the food has frozen, pop out the single serving–size portions and transfer to a freezer-safe resealable bag.

- **Purees, casseroles, and other mixed cooked foods will keep for about two months in the freezer.** Cooked meats will last a bit longer—up to three months or so. Always label your food with the date when it goes into the freezer and discard anything that may no longer be safe or of good quality.

- **To use a frozen food, first thaw it and then heat it to a safe temperature.** To thaw, place in the refrigerator overnight or defrost slowly in the microwave. Once the food has defrosted, heat it to the safe internal temperature of 165°F, then serve immediately or refrigerate. Discard leftovers after two or three days.

Although it is safe to refreeze leftovers after the food has been reheated to the safe internal temperature of 165°F, we don't recommend doing this, given the increased risk of introducing bacteria while handling the food.

[1]All storage tips are aligned with USDA guidelines.

SHAZI'S TIP

I love to use pouches for easy, on-the-go storage. Pouches have been a great way for Zane to eat our organic recipes (esp veggies), and now you can buy reusable, BPA-free pouches that you can fill yourself.

ON-THE-GO FEEDING TIPS

Packing up baby for a day out on the town? Here are some tips for keeping baby well-fed during your travels:

- **Consider the temperature.** If you're packing a cold food that will be out of the refrigerator for more than two hours, use an insulated lunch bag with two reusable ice packs to keep it nice and cold. If you plan to serve a food warm, consider the reheating options at your destination. Depending on how long you'll be out, you can heat food at home and keep it in a thermos until mealtime. Be sure to follow the manufacturer's directions for your thermos to ensure it stays hot (140°F or above) until the food is eaten.

- **Consider the best container for the job.** Spill-proof containers with properly fitting lids are the best choice for most foods.

- **Keep dips and condiments separate from foods that are dry.** For dry foods, consider reusable sandwich and snack bags, available online and at many stores.

- **Use pouches for pureed baby food on the go to avoid utensils all together!** The baby food aisle has transformed over the last decade to include dozens of baby blends and meals in this convenient packaging. You can purchase reusable, dishwasher-safe, and oven freezer-safe pouches, too.

- **Don't forget feeding accessories.** Keep your baby's spoon and/or fork in a container or a resealable bag. And, it's a good idea to have an extra one on hand in case your little one tosses his on the floor! Pack a bib made of a material, such as plastic, that can be rinsed and dried before you put it back in your bag.

- **Portable place mats can be very helpful once baby is self-feeding.** Plastic or silicone mats are nice because they tend to stick to a table and can be rinsed and wiped before they are repacked.

- **For leftovers, save food only if you have a way to keep it chilled at a safe temperature.** When in doubt, throw it out.

STORING FOOD FOR TODDLERS

When your child begins to eat some of the same types of food that you also enjoy, you can store leftovers using the same methods you employ for your own meals. Since many things can affect the amount your toddler eats on any occasion, it's nice to know that any of the toddler recipes in this cookbook will easily store in the refrigerator for two to three days. Many of the recipes in the latter portion of this book make enough to feed the whole family.

1
Simple Baby Purees
4+ MONTHS, STARTING SOLIDS

Before six months of age, breast milk or infant formula provides all the nutrition your baby needs. That means that eating is really more about flavors, textures, motor skills, and fun than nutrition. Babies are just beginning to test the limits of their sensory development and may or may not be ready to taste and touch and smell their new food with gusto. No doubt you'll know what their nose and taste buds like (and don't like!) very quickly. Remember that breast milk and/or baby formula still supplies the most complete form of nutrition to infants at this stage, and there is no need to leave it out of your baby's first experience with baby food. Use it to thin purees to the consistency preferred by your baby.

Carrots ARE A GREAT *first food* BECAUSE THEY ARE *healthy & easy* TO DIGEST.

STEAMED VEGETABLE PUREES

Steaming vegetables helps to retain the nutritional value of fresh veggies. Always remember to wash veggies, even if they will be peeled before steaming. Removing the peel from carrots does not impact their nutritional value. Most of their nutrients lie just below the skin.

INGREDIENTS

CHOOSE ANY ONE VEGETABLE OPTION:

10–12 green beans, trimmed and cut into 1-inch pieces

2 small to medium zucchini or yellow summer squash, cut into 1-inch pieces (about 1½ cups)

4 medium carrots, peeled or unpeeled, and cut into 1-inch pieces (about 2 cups)

4–5 cups chopped Swiss chard (leaves coarsely chopped, stalks finely chopped; see Note)

Breast milk or formula, as needed

1 tablespoon unsalted butter

MAKES ABOUT 1½ CUPS

DIRECTIONS

1 Fill a pot with 2 inches of water and bring to a boil over high heat. Put the vegetables in a steamer basket and place in the pot. Cover and steam until tender, about 7 minutes for green beans and zucchini, 8 minutes for carrots, and 3–5 minutes for chard. Remove the steamer basket and let the vegetables cool. Reserve the steaming liquid.

2 Working with one vegetable at a time, transfer the vegetables to a food processor or blender and puree until smooth. Add the reserved steaming liquid or breast milk, 1 tablespoon at a time, if needed to thin the puree; it should pour easily and have a consistency slightly thicker than heavy cream. Blend in the butter until melted.

3 Serve immediately. To store, refrigerate in an airtight container for up to 2 days, or freeze in individual portions (see page 16) for up to 3 months.

NOTE

It's best to wait until baby is at least six months old to introduce dark leafy greens so she can digest them. But when you start, don't overlook Swiss chard. It's just as nutritious as kale and spinach. It's part of the beet family and has vitamins A and C, as well as magnesium, potassium, and iron. Select red Swiss chard or rainbow chard, which are sweeter than the white-stalked variety.

VEGETARIAN   EGG-FREE   GLUTEN-FREE   NUT-FREE   DAIRY-FREE

TROPICAL FRUIT PUREES

Ripe tropical fruits do not need to be cooked because they have enzymes that can help baby digest. Their flesh contains vitamin C, which helps support a healthy immune system, and vitamin A, which assists with vision development.

INGREDIENTS

CHOOSE ANY ONE FRUIT OPTION:

1 ripe mango, peeled, flesh cut from pit into small chunks

1 ripe papaya, peeled, seeded, and cut into small chunks

Breast milk, formula, or water, as needed

MAKES ½–¾ CUP

 NOTE

For a variation, add melon to this fruity mix. Honeydew, cantaloupe, and watermelon all yield tasty, refreshing, and colorful purees.

DIRECTIONS

1 Place the mango or papaya chunks in a food processor or blender and puree until smooth. Add the breast milk, 1 tablespoon at a time, if needed to thin the puree; it should pour easily and have a consistency slightly thicker than heavy cream.

2 Serve immediately. To store, refrigerate in an airtight container for up to 2 days, or freeze in individual portions (see page 16) for up to 3 months.

WHEN *frozen,* THESE *fruit purees* PROVIDE BABY WITH SWEET RELIEF WHEN TEETH START COMING IN!

VEGETARIAN EGG-FREE GLUTEN-FREE NUT-FREE

ROASTED VEGETABLE PUREES

Winter squash, sweet potatoes, and beets are good choices for roasting. The oven's dry heat concentrates the flavors and brings out the sweetness in their dense flesh, resulting in a rich and naturally sweet puree. Since it's easy to roast vegetables separately on the same pan, cook three vegetables at once and puree them one at a time. Store them to use as needed.

INGREDIENTS

CHOOSE ONE OR MORE VEGETABLE OPTIONS:

2 sweet potatoes, scrubbed and pricked in a few places with a fork

1 small winter squash (such as butternut, acorn, or delicata), ends trimmed, halved, and seeded

5–6 medium red or golden beets, ends trimmed and scrubbed

Breast milk, formula, or water, as needed

1 tablespoon unsalted butter

MAKES ABOUT 2 CUPS

DIRECTIONS

1 Preheat the oven to 400°F. Line a baking dish or baking sheet with parchment paper. Place the vegetables in a single layer on the prepared baking dish, cut sides down if halved. If roasting beets, place another layer of parchment over the top, then cover with aluminum foil, folding the foil over the pan rim to seal.

2 Roast the vegetables until very tender when pierced with a fork, 45–60 minutes. Let cool for 10–20 minutes.

3 Cut sweet potatoes in half. For the sweet potatoes and winter squash, scoop the flesh from the skins with a spoon. For the beets, remove the skins by rubbing them off with a paper towel or peeling them with a paring knife, then cut the beets into chunks.

4 Working with one vegetable at a time, transfer to a food processor or blender and puree until smooth. Add the breast milk, 1 tablespoon at a time, if needed to thin the puree; it should pour easily and have a consistency slightly thicker than heavy cream. Blend in the butter until melted.

5 Serve immediately. To store, refrigerate in separate airtight containers for up to 2 days, or freeze in individual portions (see page 16) for up to 3 months.

STEAMED FRUIT PUREES

Fruits that contain pectin, such as apples, pears, peaches, nectarines, and plums, should be cooked before feeding to babies younger than six months. Cooking these fruits helps to break down the pectin, making it easier for baby to digest. Try different combinations of fruits, such as plum and peach or apple and pear.

INGREDIENTS

CHOOSE ANY ONE FRUIT OPTION:

2 peaches, skin on, pitted, and cut into chunks

2 nectarines, peeled, pitted, and cut into chunks

2 plums, peeled, pitted, and cut into chunks

2 apples, peeled, cored, and cut into chunks

2 pears, peeled, cored, and cut into chunks

Breast milk or formula, as needed

MAKES ABOUT 1 CUP

DIRECTIONS

1 Fill a pot with 2 inches of water and bring to a boil over high heat. Arrange fruit in a steamer basket and place in the pot. Cover and steam until very tender, 5–10 minutes. Remove the steamer basket and let the fruit cool. Reserve the steaming liquid.

2 Transfer the fruit to a food processor or blender and puree until smooth. Add the reserved steaming liquid or breast milk, 1 tablespoon at a time, if needed to thin the puree; it should pour easily and have a consistency similar to smooth applesauce.

3 Serve immediately. To store, refrigerate in an airtight container for up to 2 days, or freeze in individual portions (see page 16) for up to 3 months.

SWITCH IT UP

- *After baby becomes accustomed to plain cooked fruit puree, you can spice it up to help expand baby's palate. For a ½-cup serving of fruit puree, add just a pinch of a single type of ground spice, such as allspice, cardamom, cinnamon, cloves, ginger, or nutmeg.*

AVOCADO & BANANA MASHES

Bananas and avocados are convenient first foods for babies since they don't need to be cooked prior to eating. Ripe bananas contain the enzyme amylase, which is helpful to digestion. Avocados are a "good fat" food beneficial to baby's brain and physical development.

INGREDIENTS

CHOOSE ANY ONE FRUIT OPTION:

1 very ripe banana (with brown spots), peeled

1 ripe avocado, halved and pitted

Breast milk, formula, or water, as needed

MAKES ½–¾ CUP

DIRECTIONS

1 Place the banana into a small bowl, or scoop the avocado flesh from the skin into a small bowl. Mash the banana or avocado with a fork or the back of a spoon until smooth. Add breast milk to thin the puree to the consistency your baby can handle.

2 Serve immediately. To store, transfer the puree to an airtight container (placing a damp paper towel directly over the surface of the avocado puree), cover, and refrigerate for up to 1 day. The banana puree can also be frozen in individual portions (see page 16) for up to 3 months. (Some slight discoloration may occur during storage.)

SHAZI'S TIP

Avocado was Zane's very first food. I wanted to start with something that was not too high in sugar and contained healthy fats. We then began to add a small amount of banana to the avocado, and the sweetness really made my boy smile.

EGG-FREE

GLUTEN-FREE

NUT-FREE

MEAT PUREES

Meat contains lots of protein and iron, as well as B vitamins, which boost baby's energy. Select meats and poultry that are pasture raised and/or organic—they are more nutritious and will minimize potential exposure to artificial hormones, which are not allowed in organic meats. As a nutritious addition to any meat puree, or even egg yolk, try shaving freeze-dried liver into the recipe.

INGREDIENTS

½ lb beef, lamb, or chicken

½–1 cup beef broth, chicken broth, or water

1 tablespoon unsalted butter

Pinch of unrefined sea salt (Celtic or Himalayan)

MAKES 1–1½ CUPS

DIRECTIONS

1 For beef or lamb puree, bring a saucepan half full of water to a boil over high heat. Add the meat, reduce the heat to medium-low, and simmer until tender, about 1 hour.

For chicken puree, place the chicken in a saucepan and add ½ cup chicken broth. Bring to a boil over high heat. Reduce the heat to medium-low and simmer until the meat is cooked through and no longer pink in the center, 30–35 minutes.

2 Transfer the meat to a food processor or blender. Add ½ cup beef broth if pureeing beef or lamb, or transfer both the chicken and the cooking liquid if pureeing chicken. Add the butter and salt; puree until smooth. Add additional broth to thin the puree to the consistency your baby can handle.

3 Serve immediately. To store, refrigerate in an airtight container for up to 2 days, or freeze in individual portions (see page 16) for up to 1 month.

EGG YOLK

Egg yolks are an ideal first complementary food for babies as they are easy to digest and include over 100 mg choline as well as vitamin A, iron, and calcium. They also contain cholesterol, which is necessary to protect the nervous system and brain and to metabolize vitamin D. Egg yolks, unlike the whites, do not contain any of the proteins that can cause an allergic reaction in those sensitive to dairy.

INGREDIENTS

1 large egg, preferably organic pasture-raised or cage-free

Pinch of salt

MAKES 1 SERVING

SHAZI'S TIP

Egg yolk is a typical first food from the Weston A. Price philosophy which, like our Enlightened Nutrition Philosophy, focuses on restoring nutrient-rich foods to diets. Some moms are hesitant to give their babies an egg yolk, but Zane loved it as one of his first foods.

DIRECTIONS

1. Fill a small saucepan with water and bring to a boil over medium-high heat. Using a slotted spoon, gently lower the egg into the water, reduce the heat to low, and simmer until soft-boiled, 4–5 minutes. Using the spoon, remove the egg from the pan and rinse with cold running water.

2. Crack the eggshell and peel it off. Cut the egg in half and scoop out the yolk, discarding the egg white or saving for another use. Add the salt and serve immediately.

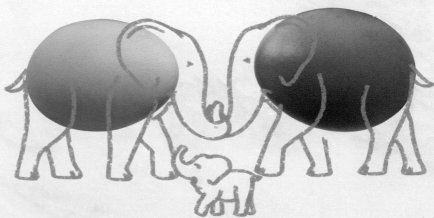

2
Baby Meals

6+ MONTHS, FLAVORFUL COMBOS

Did you know that babies have more
taste buds than adults? Luckily, these little taste
receptors are highly adaptable. In fact, research
shows that the more times babies are exposed
to a food or a flavor, the more likely they are to
accept it and even develop a preference
for it. So, during this stage, when your baby
is learning to eat new foods and textures, you
have a great opportunity to teach her to love
delicious, wholesome foods! The recipes in
this section provide a wide variety of nutrient-rich
ingredients and fresh flavors to grow on.

Rinse blueberries well, AS YOU WOULD FOR ANY FRESH FOOD, *before cooking them.*

VEGETARIAN   EGG-FREE   GLUTEN-FREE   NUT-FREE   DAIRY-FREE

BANANA, BEET & BLUEBERRY PUREE

Banana, beet, and blueberry is a fun combination of flavors (to say and to eat) that produces a puree with a rich and vibrant hue. This is one of our original recipes and has been a best seller for years. It also freezes nicely in a popsicle tray for older children to enjoy.

INGREDIENTS

1 large beet, scrubbed, peeled, and chopped

2 cups blueberries, fresh or frozen

2 ripe bananas, peeled and sliced

Breast milk or formula, as needed

MAKES 4 CUPS

SHAZI'S TIP

This gorgeous puree is one of our all-time favorite pouch recipes at Happy Family. When time is short, I substitute canned beets for the fresh ones in this (or any!) recipe.

DIRECTIONS

1 Fill a pot with 2 inches of water and bring to a boil over high heat. Put the beet in a steamer basket and place in the pot. Cover and steam until tender, about 15 minutes, adding more water to the pot as needed. Distribute the blueberries and bananas over the beets in the steamer basket. Cover and cook until tender, 2–3 minutes. Remove the steamer basket and let the vegetables and fruits cool. Reserve the steaming liquid.

2 Place the beet, blueberries, and bananas in a food processor or blender and puree until smooth. Add the reserved steaming liquid or breast milk, 1 tablespoon at a time, if needed to thin the puree; it should pour easily and have a consistency similar to smooth applesauce.

3 Serve immediately. To store, refrigerate in an airtight container for up to 2 days, or freeze in individual portions (see page 16) for up to 3 months.

VEGETARIAN   EGG-FREE   NUT-FREE   DAIRY-FREE

APPLE, BLUEBERRY & OAT PUREE

Inspired by one of our newest products, this speedy recipe is made with old-fashioned oats. It's a great option for breakfast but without all the added sugar found in most quick-cooking oatmeal packets. The apples and blueberries provide sweetness, as well as fiber and vitamin C.

INGREDIENTS

2 apples

½ cup blueberries, fresh or frozen

¾ cup old-fashioned oats

MAKES 2 CUPS

DIRECTIONS

1 Peel and core the apples and cut into chunks. Wash the blueberries.

2 Place the apples and blueberries into a saucepan with ¼ cup water. Simmer on low heat for 2–3 minutes until the apples are tender when pierced with a fork and the blueberries have burst open.

3 To cook the oats, bring 1½ cups water to a boil in a small saucepan. Stir in the oats and reduce the heat to medium. Cook, stirring occasionally, until the oats are slightly creamy, about 5 minutes (or cook as directed on the package).

4 In a food processor or blender, puree the apples, blueberries, and oats until smooth. Let cool before serving. To store, refrigerate in an airtight container for up to 2 days, or freeze in individual portions (see page 16) for up to 3 months.

VEGETARIAN EGG-FREE GLUTEN-FREE NUT-FREE DAIRY-FREE

SPINACH, MANGO & PEAR PUREE

Featuring three great flavors, this tasty blend has been a consistent favorite among Happy Family customers. Its delicious mix of spinach and fruits proves a winning combination babies enjoy. You can use either fresh or frozen spinach for this recipe.

INGREDIENTS

1 teaspoon extra-virgin olive oil

1¼ cups firmly packed fresh baby spinach, or 1 package (10 oz) frozen baby spinach, defrosted and squeezed dry

2 ripe mangoes, peeled, flesh cut from pits into small chunks

1 pear, peeled, cored, and cut into small chunks

¼–½ cup breast milk, formula, or water, as needed

MAKES 3 CUPS

DIRECTIONS

1   In a small frying pan over medium-high heat, warm the olive oil. Add the spinach and cook until wilted, about 2 minutes. Pour off any moisture in the frying pan and let the spinach cool.

2   Place the spinach, mangoes, and pear in a food processor or blender and puree until smooth. Add the breast milk, 1 tablespoon at a time, if needed to thin the puree; it should pour easily and have a consistency slightly thicker than smooth applesauce.

3   Serve immediately. To store, refrigerate in an airtight container for up to 2 days, or freeze in individual portions (see page 16) for up to 3 months.

SHAZI'S TIP

This recipe is one of the first I developed in my galley kitchen in Brooklyn, when I was launching Happy Family. It has been popular ever since.

VEGETARIAN EGG-FREE GLUTEN-FREE NUT-FREE

AVOCADO, KIWI & KALE YOGURT

Babies' bodies get a real taste of goodness with this nutrient-dense blend.
This creamy green puree teems with folate from kale and vitamin C from kiwi.
Yogurt can be introduced to babies once they start on solids.

INGREDIENTS

2 cups baby kale leaves, or regular kale with stems removed and leaves chopped

1 avocado, halved, pitted, and peeled

1 kiwi, peeled and chopped

½ cup plain whole-milk Greek yogurt (see Note)

⅓ cup applesauce

2 tablespoons loosely packed fresh mint leaves

MAKES 1½ CUPS

DIRECTIONS

1 In a food processor or blender, combine the kale, avocado, kiwi, yogurt, applesauce, and mint. Puree until smooth or until the desired consistency is achieved.

2 Serve immediately. To store, refrigerate in an airtight container for up to 2 days.

NOTE

Greek yogurt is certainly gaining in popularity, and we can understand why: Greek yogurt generally contributes more protein ounce for ounce and has a thicker, creamier consistency and a slightly less-sweet taste than regular yogurt. We suggest choosing a plain, unsweetened full-fat or 2% option.

Kale IS A superfood & A TERRIFIC SOURCE OF vitamins A & C.

EGG-FREE

GLUTEN-FREE

NUT-FREE

DAIRY-FREE

HEARTY CHICKEN & VEGGIE PUREE

Protein is a key nutrient in infant development as it helps your baby receive healthy enzymes and hormones and it fuels tissue growth and repair. This high-protein puree contains a blend of both plant-based and animal-based protein sources.

INGREDIENTS

2 small sweet potatoes, peeled and diced (about 1½ cups)

1 teaspoon olive oil

½ lb ground chicken

1 cup frozen peas, defrosted

1 cup frozen lima beans, defrosted

Chicken broth or water, as needed

MAKES 1¾ CUPS

DIRECTIONS

1 Fill a pot with 2 inches of water and bring to a boil over high heat. Distribute sweet potatoes in a steamer basket and place in the pot. Cover and steam until tender, 10–12 minutes. Remove the steamer basket from the pot and let the sweet potatoes cool. Set aside.

2 In a large frying pan over medium-high heat, warm the olive oil. Add the ground chicken and ¼ cup water. Cook, breaking up the meat with a wooden spoon and stirring constantly, until the meat is opaque throughout and no longer pink, 5–6 minutes. Remove from the heat and let cool slightly.

3 Using a slotted spoon, transfer the chicken to a food processor or blender, reserving any meat juices remaining in the pan. Add the sweet potatoes, peas, lima beans, and ½ cup of the reserved meat juices, adding broth if there is not enough reserved juices. Puree until smooth or until the desired consistency is achieved.

4 Serve immediately. To store, refrigerate in an airtight container for up to 2 days, or freeze in individual portions (see page 16) for up to 3 months.

BABY'S FIRST LAMB & BARLEY

Mix up the meat offerings by giving baby a first meal of lamb. Barley is a versatile whole grain that includes an easily digestible source of energy. This blend is filled with protein, iron, and fiber. Add the meat pan juices to the puree for depth of flavor and added nutrition.

INGREDIENTS

1 teaspoon olive oil

½ lb ground lamb

½ cup cooked pearled barley

1 cup frozen peas, defrosted

2 tablespoons loosely packed fresh mint leaves

1 teaspoon chopped fresh rosemary leaves

Beef broth or water, as needed

MAKES 1¾ CUPS

DIRECTIONS

1 In a large frying pan over medium-high heat, warm the olive oil. Add the ground lamb and ¼ cup water. Cook, breaking up the meat with a wooden spoon and stirring constantly, until the meat is opaque throughout and no longer pink, 6–7 minutes. Remove from the heat and let cool slightly.

2 Using a slotted spoon, transfer the lamb to a food processor or blender, reserving any meat juices remaining in the pan. Add the barley, peas, mint, rosemary, and ¼ cup of the reserved meat juices, adding broth if there is not enough reserved juices. Puree until smooth or until the desired consistency is achieved, adding more liquid if needed.

3 Serve immediately. To store, refrigerate in an airtight container for up to 2 days, or freeze in individual portions (see page 16) for up to 3 months.

Carrots ARE ESPECIALLY EASY FOR BABY TO DIGEST.

EGG-FREE   GLUTEN-FREE   NUT-FREE   DAIRY-FREE

TURKEY, CARROT & APRICOT PUREE

Babies love this sweet and tangy puree. Turkey is a lean meat that supplies protein and vitamin B12. The carrots and dried apricots contribute antioxidant vitamin A. Reusing the cooking water from the turkey is a good way to help retain some of the nutrients.

INGREDIENTS

2 carrots, peeled and chopped (about 1 cup)

1 teaspoon olive oil

½ lb ground turkey breast

½ cup unsulfured dried apricots, cut in half

Chicken broth or water, as needed

MAKES 1½ CUPS

DIRECTIONS

1 Fill a pot with 2 inches of water and bring to a boil over high heat. Distribute the carrots in a steamer basket and place in the pot. Cover and steam until tender, 8–10 minutes. Remove the steamer basket from the pot and let the carrots cool.

2 In a large frying pan over medium-high heat, warm the olive oil. Add the ground turkey and ¼ cup water. Cook, breaking up the meat with a wooden spoon and stirring constantly, until the meat is opaque throughout and no longer pink, 5–6 minutes. Remove from the heat and let cool slightly.

3 Using a slotted spoon, transfer the turkey to a food processor or blender, reserving any meat juices remaining in the pan. Add the carrots, apricots, and ¼ cup of the reserved meat juices, adding broth if there is not enough reserved juices. Puree until smooth or until the desired consistency is achieved.

4 Serve immediately. To store, refrigerate in an airtight container for up to 2 days, or freeze in individual portions (see page 16) for up to 3 months.

VEGETARIAN   EGG-FREE   GLUTEN-FREE   NUT-FREE   DAIRY-FREE

SPINACH, FRUIT & CHIA BLEND

In this textured puree, chia—a revered ancient seed—is blended with fruits and spinach to create a dish with antioxidant vitamins A, C, and E. Chia includes an omega-3 fatty acid (ALA), and has lots of fiber to prevent constipation, which may tempt you to take a bite yourself!

INGREDIENTS

1 cup baby spinach leaves

1 cup blueberries, fresh or frozen

1 ripe banana, peeled

1 ripe mango, peeled, pitted, and diced

1 tablespoon chia seeds

¾ cup cooked brown rice

MAKES 3 CUPS

DIRECTIONS

1 In a food processor or blender, combine the spinach, blueberries, banana, mango, chia seeds, and rice. Puree until smooth or until the desired consistency is achieved.

2 Serve immediately. To store, refrigerate in an airtight container for up to 2 days, or freeze in individual portions (see page 16) for up to 3 months.

SHAZI'S TIP

I fed Zane this antioxidant blend during those winter months when everyone seemed to be succumbing to colds and flu and I wanted to fortify him as much as possible. Feeding your baby this blend can boost his immature immune system and offers you the peace of mind that you are giving your little one the best defense against the big bad outside world.

Chia ACTS AS A *natural* THICKENER FOR A *pudding-like* CONSISTENCY.

VEGETARIAN EGG-FREE GLUTEN-FREE NUT-FREE DAIRY-FREE

PEACHY PEAR & QUINOA PUREE

Babies love the sweet flavors of peach and pear, and the vanilla adds an extra twist for tiny taste buds. The peaches and quinoa provide the antioxidant vitamin E. Opt for an iron-fortified quinoa for added nutritional benefit.

INGREDIENTS

⅓ cup quinoa

1 teaspoon vanilla extract

1 fresh peach, skin on, pitted, and cut into chunks, or 1 cup frozen sliced peaches, defrosted

1 pear, peeled, cored, and chopped

MAKES 2 CUPS

DIRECTIONS

1 Rinse the quinoa under cold running water and drain well. In a small saucepan, combine the quinoa with ⅔ cup water and the vanilla. Bring to a boil over high heat. Cover, reduce heat to low, and simmer until tender and most of the liquid has been absorbed, about 15 minutes. Remove from the heat and let stand, covered, for 10 minutes. Fluff with a fork.

2 In a food processor or blender, combine the quinoa with the peach and pear. Puree until smooth or until the desired consistency is achieved.

3 Serve immediately. To store, refrigerate in an airtight container for up to 2 days, or freeze in individual portions (see page 16) for up to 3 months.

EGG-FREE · GLUTEN-FREE · NUT-FREE · DAIRY-FREE

TURKEY, BUTTERNUT SQUASH & PEACH PUREE

Peaches and squash have a sweet flavor profile that babies adore. They help your little one receive vitamins A and C for eye and skin health. Turkey adds protein to the mix.

INGREDIENTS

½ small butternut squash, peeled, seeded, and cubed (about 1 cup)

1 teaspoon olive oil

½ lb ground turkey

¼ fresh peach, skin on, pitted, and cut into chunks, or ¼ cup frozen sliced peaches, defrosted (see Note)

⅛ teaspoon ground cinnamon

⅛ teaspoon ground ginger

MAKES 1¼ CUPS

 NOTE

It's helpful to keep a few frozen fruits and veggies on hand to use when you don't have fresh produce. We prefer frozen produce over canned—the nutrient level is higher.

DIRECTIONS

1 Fill a pot with 2 inches of water and bring to a boil over high heat. Distribute the squash in a steamer basket and place in the pot. Cover and steam until tender, 10–12 minutes. Remove the steamer basket from the pot and let the squash cool slightly.

2 In a large frying pan over medium-high heat, warm the olive oil. Add the turkey and ¼ cup water. Cook, breaking up the turkey with a wooden spoon and stirring constantly, until the meat is opaque throughout and no longer pink, 5–6 minutes. Remove from the heat and let cool slightly.

3 Using a slotted spoon, transfer the turkey to a food processor or blender, reserving any meat juices remaining in the pan. Add the squash, peach, cinnamon, and ginger. Puree until smooth, adding as much of the reserved meat juices as needed to achieve the desired consistency.

4 Serve immediately. To store, refrigerate in an airtight container for up to 2 days, or freeze in individual portions (see page 16) for up to 3 months.

Carrots ADD A NATURAL SWEETNESS THAT BABIES LOVE!

VEGETARIAN   EGG-FREE   GLUTEN-FREE   NUT-FREE   DAIRY-FREE

CARROT, PEACH, AVOCADO & FLAXSEED PUREE

This puree is an adventure for tiny taste buds. The ground flaxseeds contribute omega-3 (ALA) and polyunsaturated fatty acids. The avocado contains beneficial monounsaturated fats. Intake of dietary fats is important for infant growth.

INGREDIENTS

2 carrots, peeled and chopped (about 1 cup)

1 fresh peach, skin on, pitted, and chopped, or 1 cup frozen sliced peaches, defrosted

1 avocado, halved, pitted, and peeled

1 teaspoon ground flaxseeds

¼ teaspoon ground ginger

MAKES 1½ CUPS

DIRECTIONS

1 Fill a pot with 2 inches of water and bring to a boil over high heat. Distribute carrots in a steamer basket and place in the pot. Cover and steam until tender, 8–10 minutes. Remove the steamer basket from the pot and let the carrots cool.

2 In a food processor or blender, combine the carrots, peach, avocado, flaxseeds, and ginger. Puree until smooth or until the desired consistency is achieved.

3 Serve immediately. To store, refrigerate in an airtight container for up to 2 days, or freeze in individual portions (see page 16) for up to 3 months.

VEGETARIAN · EGG-FREE · GLUTEN-FREE · NUT-FREE · DAIRY-FREE

STRAWBERRY, AVOCADO & BEET BLEND

Vitamin C is a water-soluble vitamin that is particularly important when starting baby on solids, since it helps the body absorb iron. This beautiful pinkish blend contains antioxidants from vitamins C and E as well as good fats.

INGREDIENTS

2 beets, scrubbed (see Note)

1 avocado, halved, pitted, and peeled

1 cup hulled and halved strawberries

MAKES 1¾ CUPS

DIRECTIONS

1 Bring a pot of salted water to a boil over high heat. Add the beets and cook until tender, about 45 minutes. Drain. Fill the pot with cold water and return the beets to the pot. Holding the beets under the water, peel off the skins and discard. Halve the beets and transfer to a food processor or blender. Add the avocado and strawberries. Puree until smooth or until the desired consistency is achieved.

2 Serve immediately. To store, refrigerate in an airtight container for up to 2 days, or freeze in individual portions (see page 16) for up to 3 months.

 NOTE

You can use unsalted, canned, or vacuum-packed beets instead of cooking your own.

Sliced strawberries HAVE MORE vitamin C THAN ORANGES, cup for cup!

VEGETARIAN

EGG-FREE

GLUTEN-FREE

NUT-FREE

DAIRY-FREE

GREEN BEAN & LENTIL BLEND

Simple but intriguing, this blend of legumes and aromatic spices serves up plant-based protein and iron to help support growth and development. Cardamom and cinnamon not only flavor the dish but also leave your kitchen smelling like a spice market.

INGREDIENTS

½ lb green beans, trimmed

½ cup small green or brown lentils

⅛ teaspoon ground cinnamon

Pinch of ground cardamom

MAKES ABOUT 2 CUPS

SHAZI'S TIP

I grew up eating foods flavored with cardamom, one of the world's ancient spices from the East. My mom used it in dishes made with legumes (seeds that grow within pods, like peas, lentils, and chickpeas), in curries, and even in sweet desserts.

DIRECTIONS

1 Fill a pot with 2 inches of water and bring to a boil over high heat. Distribute the green beans in a steamer basket and place in the pot. Cover and steam until tender, 7–8 minutes. Remove the steamer basket from the pot and let the green beans cool.

2 Pick over the lentils for stones or grit. Rinse in a colander and drain thoroughly. Bring a pot of water to a boil over high heat. Add the lentils, reduce the heat to low, and simmer until tender, 18–20 minutes. Drain.

3 In a food processor or blender, combine the green beans, lentils, cinnamon, and cardamom. Puree until smooth or until the desired consistency is achieved.

4 Serve immediately. To store, refrigerate in an airtight container for up to 2 days, or freeze in individual portions (see page 16) for up to 3 months.

VEGETARIAN   EGG-FREE   GLUTEN-FREE   NUT-FREE DAIRY-FREE

VEGETABLE MEDLEY

This four-vegetable puree is a great way to incorporate fresh ingredients. Featuring calcium, vitamins A and E, and support for eye and skin health, this vibrant medley also has a tasty combination of flavors thanks to the sage, nutmeg, and ginger.

INGREDIENTS

1 cup green beans, trimmed

1 cup chopped cauliflower florets

1 cup baby spinach leaves

1 cup canned pumpkin puree

½ teaspoon ground sage

⅛ teaspoon ground nutmeg

⅛ teaspoon ground ginger

MAKES 2 CUPS

DIRECTIONS

1 Fill a pot with 2 inches of water and bring to a boil over high heat. Distribute the green beans and cauliflower in a steamer basket and place in the pot. Cover and steam until tender, 7–8 minutes. Remove the steamer basket from the pot and let the vegetables cool.

2 In a food processor or blender, combine the green beans and cauliflower with the spinach, pumpkin, sage, nutmeg, and ginger. Puree until smooth or until the desired consistency is achieved.

3 Serve immediately. To store, refrigerate in an airtight container for up to 2 days, or freeze in individual portions (see page 16) for up to 3 months.

SHAZI'S TIP

I always keep a bag of spinach in the freezer as a standby. (Just be sure to drain it well before using.) Flash-frozen vegetables and fruits are nutritious—the next best thing to buying local produce!

Quinoa IS A **complete** protein, CONTAINING **all 9** OF THE *essential* amino acids.

BLACKBERRY, BANANA, PEACH & QUINOA PUREE

Blackberries are known to deliver antioxidants, which adds a nice balance to bananas that contain potassium and peaches with vitamin C. Quinoa leads the way with its naturally gluten-free goodness and protein. Tiny blackberry seeds give this puree a bit of texture; use a fine-mesh strainer to remove them if you prefer.

INGREDIENTS

1½ ripe bananas, peeled

1 cup blackberries

1 fresh peach, skin on, pitted, and cut into chunks, or 1 cup frozen sliced peaches, defrosted

½ cup cooked quinoa

2 tablespoons loosely packed fresh basil leaves (see Note)

MAKES 2½ CUPS

DIRECTIONS

1 In a food processor or blender, combine the bananas, blackberries, peach, quinoa, and basil. Puree until smooth or until the desired consistency is achieved.

2 Serve immediately. To store, refrigerate in an airtight container for up to 2 days, or freeze in individual portions (see page 16) for up to 3 months. (Some discoloration may occur during prolonged storage.)

NOTE

It may seem odd putting basil into your baby's puree. But basil is much more than a flavorful herb—it's a vitamin K powerhouse, helping build healthy bones and supporting the circulatory system. As for the flavor, it is subtle.

VEGETARIAN EGG-FREE GLUTEN-FREE NUT-FREE

CARROT-CINNAMON BROWN RICE WITH YOGURT

Stimulate your baby's senses with this sweet, lightly spiced puree. It boasts beta-carotene, protein, fiber, and vitamin B6, as well as the calcium, phosphorus, and magnesium that are beneficial for growth and the formation of bones. Both cinnamon and cumin give baby a taste of something unique.

INGREDIENTS

3 carrots, peeled and chopped (about 1½ cups)

½ cup cooked brown rice

½ cup plain whole-milk Greek yogurt

2 tablespoons raisins

¼ teaspoon ground cinnamon

⅛ teaspoon ground cumin

MAKES 1¼ CUPS

DIRECTIONS

1 Fill a pot with 2 inches of water and bring to a boil over high heat. Distribute the carrots in a steamer basket and place in the pot. Cover and steam until tender, 8–10 minutes. Remove the steamer basket from the pot and let the carrots cool.

2 In a food processor or blender, combine the carrots, rice, yogurt, raisins, cinnamon, and cumin. Puree until smooth or until the desired consistency is achieved.

3 Serve immediately. To store, refrigerate in an airtight container for up to 2 days.

SWITCH IT UP

- *If your child is dairy-free, use an unsweetened Greek-style coconut yogurt in place of regular yogurt. Naturally lactose-free, it complements the flavor profile and provides healthy fats and B vitamins.*

Spices LIKE *cinnamon* HELP EXPAND YOUR BABY'S *palate*.

VEGETARIAN   EGG-FREE   GLUTEN-FREE   NUT-FREE   DAIRY-FREE

APPLE, CANNELLINI BEAN & PRUNE PUREE

Babies are sure to love this super-sweet and healthful puree. The white beans contribute protein to this tasty concoction as well as magnesium, a mineral that promotes growth during this adventurous period of life. Prunes are legendary for keeping your baby's tummy happy.

INGREDIENTS

1 can (15 oz) cannellini beans, rinsed and drained

1 red apple, cored and chopped

1 fresh peach, skin on, pitted, and chopped, or 1 cup frozen sliced peaches, defrosted

½ cup pitted prunes, halved

2 tablespoons applesauce

MAKES 2½ CUPS

DIRECTIONS

1 In a food processor or blender, combine the beans, apple, peach, prunes, and applesauce. Puree until smooth or until the desired consistency is achieved.

2 Serve immediately. To store, refrigerate in an airtight container for up to 2 days, or freeze in individual portions (see page 16) for up to 3 months.

SWITCH IT UP

- *Substitute any bean variety that you have on hand for the cannellini beans. All varieties of edible beans—white, black, kidney, navy, and pinto, to name just a few—are packed with nutrition. In addition to protein, they are excellent sources of fiber and are fat-, sodium-, and cholesterol-free.*

SAVORY RICE PUDDING WITH PAPAYA, WHITE BEANS & SPINACH

A blend of brown rice, beans, fruit, and spinach creates outstandingly nutritious food for your little one. Papaya, vibrant with vitamin C, enhances absorption of the iron from the spinach and white beans, while the combo of rice and beans comprises a complete protein.

INGREDIENTS

2 cups peeled, seeded, and chopped papaya (see Note)

2 cups baby spinach leaves

1 can (15 oz) white beans, rinsed and drained

½ cup cooked brown rice

MAKES 2 ¾ CUPS

DIRECTIONS

1 In a food processor or a blender, combine the papaya, spinach, beans, and rice. Puree until smooth or until the desired consistency is achieved.

2 Serve immediately. To store, refrigerate in an airtight container for up to 2 days, or freeze in individual portions (see page 16) for up to 3 months.

NOTE

Mexican papaya is among the larger forms of the fruit and is more commonly found in grocery stores. Although the Mexican variety can be used in this recipe, Caribbean papaya is preferred both for its more intense sweetness and compact size. You can also try this dish using mango.

EGG-FREE

GLUTEN-FREE

NUT-FREE

SALMON WITH KALE & YOGURT

Go seaside with salmon! It is a nutrient powerhouse with high-quality protein, as well as omega-3 fatty acids (EPA and DHA) for brain, nerve, and eye health as infants continue to grow. The yogurt and kale together have calcium to help build strong bones.

INGREDIENTS

½ lb salmon fillet

2 tablespoons raisins

3 cups chopped kale leaves (stems removed)

½ cup plain whole-milk Greek yogurt

½ teaspoon dried dill

MAKES 2 CUPS

SHAZI'S TIP

In our house, we try to eat salmon at least once a week. The extra omega-3s and healthy fats are good for the whole family. Use leftovers as a great sandwich spread for adults. I've even added gluten-free bread crumbs to make fish cake patties (or you could use any type of potato, quinoa, or wild rice instead of bread crumbs).

DIRECTIONS

1 Preheat the oven to 350°F. Place the salmon, skin side down, in a baking dish. Bake until opaque throughout, about 15 minutes. Let cool. Remove the skin and discard. Separate the fish into smaller pieces. Set aside.

2 Meanwhile, place the raisins in a bowl. Add enough boiling water to cover. Let stand until the raisins are plump, 10–15 minutes. Drain.

3 Fill a pot with 2 inches of water and bring to a boil over high heat. Distribute the kale in a steamer basket and place in the pot. Cover and steam for 5 minutes. Uncover and stir gently. Continue to steam, covered, for 3 minutes longer. Remove from heat.

4 In a food processor or blender, combine the salmon, raisins, kale, yogurt, and dill. Puree until smooth or until the desired consistency is achieved.

5 Serve immediately. To store, refrigerate in an airtight container for up to 2 days.

VEGETARIAN

EGG-FREE

NUT-FREE

TROPICAL OATMEAL

Feed baby a great balance of protein, carbohydrates, and fat—as well as vitamin B6, magnesium, and vitamin C—in this sweet puree. The oats are a great source of easily digestible whole grain.

INGREDIENTS

1 cup cooked oatmeal

½ cup plain whole-milk Greek yogurt

½ cup chopped fresh pineapple

½ cup peeled and chopped mango

MAKES ABOUT 2 CUPS

DIRECTIONS

1 In a food processor or blender, combine the oatmeal, yogurt, pineapple, and mango. Puree until smooth or until the desired consistency is achieved.

2 Serve immediately. To store, refrigerate in an airtight container for up to 2 days.

SWITCH IT UP

- *Try this recipe with coconut yogurt or any flavored yogurt that your baby loves to eat.*

VEGETARIAN   EGG-FREE   GLUTEN-FREE   NUT-FREE

APRICOT & SPINACH YOGURT

The ingredients in this wholesome blend provide an array of nutrients. Babies will benefit from the high levels of antioxidants in vitamins A and E, which help to fight inflammation, while the yogurt provides a source of calcium and phosphorus to help support bone health.

INGREDIENTS

3 cups baby spinach leaves

⅓ cup plain whole-milk Greek yogurt

¼ cup dried unsulfured apricots

¼ cup raisins

½ teaspoon dried dill or a few sprigs fresh dill
(see Tip)

MAKES 1¾ CUPS

DIRECTIONS

1 In a food processor or blender, combine the spinach, yogurt, apricots, raisins, and dill. Puree until smooth or until the desired consistency is achieved.

2 Serve immediately. To store, refrigerate in an airtight container for up to 2 days.

SHAZI'S TIP

I love using fresh herbs like dill, basil, and flat-leaf parsley because they're so much more aromatic and flavorful than dried ones. I simply wrap them in a damp paper towel and store them in a baggie in the fridge.

EGG-FREE

GLUTEN-FREE

NUT-FREE

DAIRY-FREE

BEEF, SWEET POTATO & BROCCOLI PUREE

This hearty puree is sure to please baby's tummy with its protein, phosphorus, and magnesium. Beef includes protein and easily absorbed iron for healthy growth and development. Broccoli adds a further boost of iron.

INGREDIENTS

1 teaspoon olive oil

½ lb ground beef

1 large sweet potato, peeled and diced (about 1 cup)

1 cup chopped broccoli florets

Beef broth or water, as needed

MAKES 1¾ CUPS

NOTE

Hearty stews are perfect cold-weather food and very versatile. You can use whatever vegetables you have in the fridge, like carrots and cauliflower, or root vegetables like carrots, parsnips, and turnips. Simply use the same proportions as those in the recipe.

DIRECTIONS

1 In a large frying pan over medium heat, warm the olive oil. Add the beef and ¼ cup water. Cook, breaking up the meat with a wooden spoon and stirring constantly, until the meat is opaque throughout and no longer pink, 6–7 minutes. Let cool, then drain.

2 Fill a pot with 2 inches of water and bring to a boil over high heat. Place the sweet potatoes in a steamer basket and place in the pot. Cover and steam for 5 minutes. Distribute the broccoli over the potatoes. Cover and steam until the potatoes and broccoli are tender, 7–8 minutes longer. Remove the steamer basket and let the vegetables cool. Reserve the steaming liquid.

3 In a food processor or blender, combine the beef, sweet potato, broccoli, and ½ cup of the reserved steaming liquid, adding broth if there is not enough liquid. Puree until smooth or until the desired consistency is achieved.

4 Serve immediately. To store, refrigerate in an airtight container for up to 2 days, or freeze in individual portions (see page 16) for up to 3 months.

Naturally *sweet* & NUTRITIOUS *sweet potatoes*
MAKE A *great base* FOR MEAT & VEGETABLE MIXES.

3

Toddler Meals

12+ MONTHS, FIRST MEALS

As little ones transition from babies to active toddlers, seemingly on the go nonstop from morning till night, they will actually need more nutrients per pound of body weight than when they are older to fuel all this boundless energy. Yet their tummies are still small. That is why it is more important than ever that each meal be filled with nutrient-rich ingredients to make every bite count. Good nutrition for toddlers includes a mix of foods containing these essential nutrients: iron; protein; calcium; vitamins A, C, and D; fiber; DHA and other omega-3 fatty acids; and pre- and probiotics.

Tofu IS LOADED WITH *iron*, *protein* & *calcium* TO KEEP BONES STRONG.

VEGETARIAN   EGG-FREE   GLUTEN-FREE   NUT-FREE   DAIRY-FREE

12+
months

TOFU & VEGGIES WITH BASIL

Tofu is a versatile, low-calorie, plant-based protein and a healthful alternative to meat or poultry. This tasty toddler meal includes plant proteins, fiber, vitamin C, and vitamin K. The herbs and spices add lots of flavor and will start to expand your child's palate. And the lycopene-rich tomatoes are great for heart health.

INGREDIENTS

2 tablespoons vegetable oil

1 cup small cauliflower florets

1 small eggplant, cut into 1-inch cubes (about 2 cups)

2 large plum tomatoes, chopped

7 oz firm tofu, cut into 1-inch cubes

¼ teaspoon minced fresh ginger

¼ teaspoon ground turmeric

Juice of ½ lime

½ cup chopped fresh basil leaves

Salt and pepper

MAKES ABOUT 5 CUPS

DIRECTIONS

1   In a saucepan over medium heat, warm the vegetable oil. Add the cauliflower and eggplant and cook, stirring occasionally, until just beginning to soften, 3–5 minutes. Add the tomatoes, tofu, ginger, and turmeric and stir to combine.

2   Cover, reduce the heat to low, and cook until the cauliflower is tender, 3–5 minutes longer. Stir in the lime juice and basil. Season to taste with salt and pepper and serve warm. Store in an airtight container in the refrigerator for up to 4 days, or freeze for up to 3 months.

SWITCH IT UP

- *Serve this Asian-inspired tofu and vegetable medley over cooked brown rice, couscous, or quinoa.*

VEGETARIAN   NUT-FREE   DAIRY-FREE

SWEET POTATO & RAISIN PANCAKES

This is a sweet, fun spin on traditional potato pancakes. Sweet potatoes are rich in beta-carotene, which promotes good eye health. Cinnamon and raisins add a natural sweetness. These nutritious pancakes provide delicious fuel for growing kids!

INGREDIENTS

1 lb sweet potatoes, peeled and shredded (about 4 cups)

¾ cup raisins

⅓ cup whole-wheat flour

2 large eggs, lightly beaten

½ teaspoon ground cinnamon

Pinch of salt

Pinch of sugar

½ cup applesauce or plain whole-milk Greek yogurt (optional)

MAKES 8 PANCAKES

DIRECTIONS

1 Preheat the oven to 400°F. Lightly grease a baking sheet.

2 Wrap the shredded sweet potatoes in a clean kitchen towel and squeeze out the excess water.

3 In a large bowl, combine the sweet potatoes, raisins, flour, eggs, cinnamon, salt, and sugar and stir until well mixed.

4 Form the sweet potato mixture into 8 pancakes, each about 3½ inches in diameter. Place the pancakes on the prepared baking sheet and bake, turning once halfway through baking, until golden and crisp, about 20 minutes total. Serve warm with applesauce on the side for dipping, if using. Store in an airtight container in the refrigerator for up to 3 days, or freeze for up to 2 months.

EGG-FREE

GLUTEN-FREE

NUT-FREE

DAIRY-FREE

COCONUT MILK CHICKEN WITH BROCCOLI & SNOW PEAS

This Thai-inspired dish cooks lean protein and fiber-rich vegetables in mildly sweet, lightly creamy coconut milk. The broccoli and snow peas are filled with vitamin C, a water-soluble antioxidant vitamin that helps the immune system. The fresh basil and mint add wonderful bursts of flavor, as well as antioxidants.

INGREDIENTS

1 tablespoon vegetable oil

½ lb boneless, skinless chicken breast, cut into 1-inch cubes

Salt and pepper

½ cup 1-inch pieces chopped broccoli

½ cup snow peas, trimmed and quartered

½ cup canned unsweetened coconut milk

Juice of ½ lime

1 tablespoon chopped fresh basil leaves

1 tablespoon chopped fresh mint leaves

MAKES 2 ½ CUPS

DIRECTIONS

1 In a large frying pan over medium heat, warm the vegetable oil. Add the chicken and season lightly with salt and pepper. Cook, stirring, until lightly browned, about 5 minutes. Stir in the broccoli, snow peas, and coconut milk. Bring to a boil over high heat, then boil for 1 minute. Reduce the heat to low and cook, stirring occasionally, until the coconut milk thickens slightly, 15–18 minutes.

2 Stir in the lime juice, basil, and mint. Season to taste with salt and pepper and serve warm.

3 Store in an airtight container in the refrigerator for up to 3 days, or freeze for up to 2 months.

SWITCH IT UP

- *Served atop small bowls of freshly cooked brown rice or quinoa, this fragrant mixture makes a nutritious meal for the whole family.*

VEGETARIAN

EGG-FREE

NUT-FREE

BROCCOLI MAC & CHEESE

Even the boxed brands of macaroni and cheese on the supermarket shelves have to be cooked, so making this favorite casserole from scratch doesn't add much effort—and the results are dramatically better. Make it with or without vegetables. Broccoli and cauliflower pieces are a convenient choice because their cooking time is the same as for the pasta.

INGREDIENTS

½ lb elbow macaroni

1½ cups small broccoli and/or cauliflower florets

1 cup whole milk

¾ lb shredded sharp white Cheddar cheese (about 3 cups)

Salt and pepper

3 tablespoons grated Parmesan cheese

MAKES ABOUT 4 CUPS

DIRECTIONS

1 Preheat the oven to 350°F. Bring a pot of water to a boil over high heat. Reduce the heat to medium and add the macaroni and vegetables. Simmer until the macaroni is al dente and the vegetables are tender but not mushy, 7–10 minutes. Drain the pasta and vegetables and return them to the pot.

2 Heat the milk in a small saucepan over low heat. Add the hot milk and Cheddar cheese to the macaroni and vegetables and toss to combine. Season to taste with salt and pepper and stir again.

3 Pour the pasta mixture into an 8-inch-square glass or ceramic baking dish. Sprinkle Parmesan cheese over the top. Bake until bubbling, about 15 minutes. Let cool for 5–10 minutes before serving. Store in an airtight container in the refrigerator for up to 3 days, or freeze for up to 3 months.

GLUTEN-FREE   NUT-FREE

BAKED RICE BALLS WITH SALMON & PEAS

Cook up a fun alternative to an ordinary salmon and peas dinner! These colorful rice balls are packed with flavor and nutrients. Salmon includes lots of lean protein and is also rich in omega-3 fatty acids—beneficial fats that are needed for brain, nerve, and eye development. Salmon also contains vitamin B6, which helps sustain body energy levels, and vitamin D, which is needed for strong bones.

INGREDIENTS

¼ lb wild salmon fillet

1 cup cooked brown rice

1 cup frozen peas, defrosted

¼ cup grated Parmesan cheese

2 large eggs, beaten

1½ teaspoons dried dill

Pinch of salt (optional)

MAKES 8-10 RICE BALLS

SHAZI'S TIP

Zane, like most children, has a sweet tooth so green peas are one of my go-to vegetables. They may not be very exotic, but they are a little sweet and also full of fiber, protein, and even omega-3s. Frozen peas are tasty and retain their nutrients, so I can easily add them to recipes all year round.

DIRECTIONS

1   Preheat the oven to 350°F. Place the salmon, skin side down, in a baking dish. Bake until opaque throughout, about 15 minutes. Let cool. Remove the skin and discard. Using a fork, flake the salmon into small pieces, discarding any pin bones. Transfer the salmon to a bowl. Add the rice, peas, cheese, eggs, dill, and salt, if using, and stir until combined.

2   Line a baking sheet with parchment paper. Form about ⅓ cup of the salmon mixture into a 1½-inch ball and place it on the prepared baking sheet. Repeat with the remaining salmon mixture to form 8-10 balls. Loosely cover the balls with aluminum foil and bake until the balls are slightly firm but still gooey, 18-20 minutes. Let cool slightly and serve warm. Store in an airtight container in the refrigerator for up to 2 days, or freeze for up to 1 month. Reheat before serving.

VEGETARIAN

EGG-FREE

NUT-FREE

PASTA WITH KALE-SPINACH PESTO

Get your greens on with this pasta dish! Kale and spinach are both sources of vitamin K, an essential micronutrient for blood clotting that helps to keep those pesky cuts and bruises at bay. The basil adds a sweetness that will surely please all palates. This nourishing recipe makes enough for the whole family.

INGREDIENTS

5 oz baby spinach leaves

1 bunch kale, stems removed and leaves coarsely chopped (about 4 cups firmly packed)

½ cup firmly packed fresh basil leaves

½ cup grated Parmesan cheese

¼ cup olive oil

Juice of 1 lemon

Salt and pepper (optional)

8 oz whole-wheat pasta, cooked and drained

MAKES ABOUT 4½ CUPS

NOTE

Pesto is traditionally made with pine nuts or walnuts but, since they are a potential allergen, I've left them out here. If your child does not have a nut allergy, consider adding ¼ cup roasted walnuts for their omega-3s, or spice things up by adding 2–3 cloves of garlic to the mix.

DIRECTIONS

1 In a food processor, pulse the spinach, kale, basil, and cheese until coarsely chopped. Add the olive oil and continue to pulse until the oil is fully incorporated, scraping down the sides of the bowl with a spatula as needed. Add the lemon juice, season with salt and pepper, if using, and puree until smooth, 20–30 seconds.

2 In a large bowl, combine the pasta and the pesto. Toss until the pasta is evenly coated. Serve warm. Store in an airtight container in the refrigerator for up to 3 days, or freeze in individual portions (see page 16) for up to 3 months.

SWITCH IT UP

- *To make this dish gluten-free, use gluten-free pasta or serve the pesto over cooked rice.*

NUT-FREE

CARROT & SPINACH MEATBALLS

Give the classic meatball a nourishing makeover! There's no picking around the veggies here, since the carrots and spinach are mixed into the meat. Ground turkey is a lower-fat alternative to beef, and the veggies enhance the meatballs' beneficial nutritional profile. This dish also includes fat-soluble vitamins A and K for eye health, immunity, and blood clotting.

INGREDIENTS

1 lb ground turkey

2 large carrots, peeled and shredded (about 1 cup)

1 lb frozen spinach, defrosted and squeezed dry

¼ cup grated Parmesan cheese

⅓ cup bread crumbs

2 large eggs, lightly beaten

1½ teaspoons dried oregano

1½ teaspoons dried dill

Salt and pepper (optional)

MAKES ABOUT 40 MEATBALLS

DIRECTIONS

1 Preheat the oven to 375°F. Lightly grease a baking sheet.

2 In a large bowl, combine the turkey, carrots, spinach, cheese, bread crumbs, eggs, oregano, dill, and a pinch each of salt and pepper, if using. Mix with your hands until well combined.

3 Form about 2 tablespoons of the turkey mixture into a 1-inch ball and set it on the prepared baking sheet. Repeat with the remaining turkey mixture to form about 40 meatballs. Bake the meatballs, turning once halfway through baking, until golden brown, 20–24 minutes total. Store in an airtight container in the refrigerator for up to 4 days, or freeze for up to 4 months.

SWITCH IT UP

- *Meatballs can be served on their own with a favorite sauce or with a pasta of your choice.*
- *Make the dish gluten-free by using gluten-free bread crumbs.*

GLUTEN-FREE NUT-FREE DAIRY-FREE

ORANGE-Y BEEF & CARROT BURGERS

Looking for a better-for-you burger? Carrots, orange bell pepper, and orange zest fill these juicy, mildly sweet burgers with color, flavor, vitamin C, and beta-carotene to help build up immunity and keep baby's skin glowing. They also contain iron and protein—all in tasty, kid-friendly patties!

INGREDIENTS

1 lb ground beef

2 large carrots, peeled and shredded (about 1 cup)

½ orange bell pepper, finely diced (about ¾ cup)

Zest of 1 medium orange

1 large egg, lightly beaten

Pinch of salt

2 tablespoons vegetable oil, if frying

MAKES 10 BURGERS

SHAZI'S TIP

Just a few years ago, grass-fed organic beef was difficult to find in the grocery store. I feel lucky that my local store now has all sorts of different cuts of pasture-grazed organic beef. It's pretty great that consumers are moving the needle in the direction of healthful choices.

DIRECTIONS

1 In a large bowl, combine the beef, carrots, bell pepper, orange zest, egg, and salt. Mix with your hands until well combined. Form the beef mixture into 10 patties, each about 4 inches in diameter.

2 To fry the burgers, in a frying pan over high heat, warm the vegetable oil. Add the patties in a single layer and cook, turning once, until cooked through, about 10 minutes total. To bake the burgers, preheat the oven to 375°F. Lightly grease a baking sheet. Place the patties in a single layer on the baking sheet and bake, turning once halfway through baking, until cooked through, 8–10 minutes total.

3 Serve the burgers warm. Store leftovers in an airtight container in the refrigerator for up to 5 days, or freeze for up to 3 months.

Fusilli pasta, WITH ITS
swirly ridges, IS A GOOD SHAP
FOR little fingers TO GRASP.

VEGETARIAN   EGG-FREE   NUT-FREE

WHOLE-WHEAT PASTA PRIMAVERA WITH WHITE BEANS

Kids love pasta! The simple substitution of whole-wheat pasta for the regular variety is the fastest way to step up the nutritional content of any pasta dish. This vegetarian classic has a rainbow of colors and a variety of nutrients, including fiber, folate, iron, and protein. White beans are high in plant protein, complementing the pasta in the formation of a complete protein. Protein is essential for growth and helps to build strong muscles.

INGREDIENTS

8 oz whole-wheat fusilli pasta, cooked and drained

1 can (15 oz) white beans, rinsed and drained

1 cup frozen peas, defrosted

½ yellow bell pepper, diced (about ¾ cup)

½ red bell pepper, diced (about ¾ cup)

½ cup cubed mozzarella or grated Parmesan cheese (optional)

⅓ cup chopped fresh basil leaves

¼ cup olive oil

1½ tablespoons balsamic vinegar

Salt and pepper

MAKES ABOUT 8 CUPS

DIRECTIONS

1 In a large bowl, combine the pasta, beans, peas, bell peppers, and cheese, if using, and toss until well mixed. Stir in the basil, olive oil, and vinegar. Season to taste with salt and pepper.

2 Serve warm, at room temperature, or cold. Store leftovers in the refrigerator for up to 3 days.

SWITCH IT UP

- *Make this dish gluten-free by swapping in gluten-free pasta or using rice instead of pasta.*

- *Use any of your favorite vegetables in place of the bell peppers and peas. Green beans, broccoli florets, and grated carrots are all good choices.*

- *Add protein with cubed, baked, or grilled chicken breast.*

EGG-FREE   GLUTEN-FREE   NUT-FREE   DAIRY-FREE

COCONUT MILK SALMON WITH CAULIFLOWER & SPINACH

Incorporating healthful seafood into your child's diet is easy with this coconut milk and salmon favorite. Filled with omega-3 fatty acids, iron, fiber, and protein, this dish provides a wholesome meal for hungry toddlers, with plenty remaining to satisfy the whole family!

INGREDIENTS

1 can (13.5 oz) light unsweetened coconut milk

1 cup finely chopped cauliflower

1½ tablespoons sesame seeds

5 oz baby spinach leaves

½ lb skinless wild salmon fillet, pin bones removed, cut into 1-inch cubes

Juice of ½ lime

Salt and pepper

MAKES ABOUT 4 CUPS

SHAZI'S TIP

When I go shopping for salmon, I make sure that the salmon I purchase is wild. Confirmation of the salmon's origin can be difficult to find, but should be noted on the sign at the fish counter or on the packaging. One general tip I follow is that Atlantic salmon is generally farm raised, but Alaska and sockeye salmon are usually wild.

DIRECTIONS

1 In a large frying pan over medium heat, warm the coconut milk until it begins to steam (do not boil). Add the cauliflower and sesame seeds and cook until the cauliflower is al dente, about 3 minutes. Add the spinach, cover, and cook until wilted, about 3 minutes. Stir gently, then add the salmon. Cover and cook until the salmon is opaque throughout, about 5 minutes.

2 Stir in the lime juice. Season to taste with salt and pepper and serve warm. Store in an airtight container in the refrigerator for up to 3 days, or freeze for up to 2 months.

SWITCH IT UP

- *Spoon ½-cup servings over bowls of brown rice.*

THE *omega-3s* IN *salmon* ARE GREAT FOR *brain* & *eye development.*

EGG-FREE

GLUTEN-FREE

NUT-FREE

CHICKEN WITH BEET MASHED POTATOES & GREEN SAUCE

This dish creatively incorporates beets, a root vegetable that provides fiber, folate, potassium, and antioxidants. While folate is most known for healthy nervous-system development in the prenatal infant, it is also an important B vitamin for red blood cells. With the lean chicken protein, calcium-rich yogurt, and fiber-full potatoes and peas, this dish is a sure winner!

INGREDIENTS

½ lb boneless, skinless chicken breast

Salt and pepper

2 large russet potatoes, peeled and cut into 1-inch chunks

1 cup drained canned beets

1½ cups plain whole-milk Greek yogurt

2⅔ cups frozen peas, defrosted

MAKES ABOUT 4 CUPS

DIRECTIONS

1 Preheat the oven to 375°F. Lightly grease a small baking dish. Place the chicken breast in the prepared baking dish and season with salt and pepper. Cover the dish with aluminum foil and bake until the chicken is opaque throughout or until an instant-read thermometer inserted into the thickest part of the breast registers 165°F, about 30 minutes. Let the chicken cool slightly, then cut into slices about ¾ inch thick and set aside. (For younger toddlers, cut the cooked chicken into ½-inch cubes instead.)

2 Meanwhile, bring a saucepan three-fourths full of water to a boil over high heat. Add the potatoes and cook until tender, 10–12 minutes. Drain, then transfer to a bowl. Add the beets and yogurt. Using a potato masher or ricer, mash the potato mixture until smooth and thoroughly combined. Set aside. Using a food processor, puree the peas until smooth, about 10 seconds .

3 For each serving, spoon a dollop of beet mashed potatoes onto a plate, lay a few chicken slices on top, and dot with some pea puree. Store in an airtight container in the refrigerator for up to 2 days.

VEGETARIAN

EGG-FREE

GLUTEN-FREE

NUT-FREE

DAIRY-FREE

12+
months

BROWN RICE & LENTILS WITH GREEN BEANS

This vegetarian one-pot wonder simmers up in a snap and is a delicious, wholesome dish filled with nutrients, including folate, fiber, iron, phosphorus, and protein. The pairing of rice and lentils makes a complete protein. Lentils are an excellent and economical way to get both protein and fiber into the body. This generous recipe makes enough for a family supper.

INGREDIENTS

1¼ cups brown rice

1 cup brown lentils

8 oz green beans, cut into ½-inch lengths

1 can (14.5 oz) crushed tomatoes

½ teaspoon ground cinnamon

1 tablespoon dried oregano

Salt

⅔ cup unsweetened dried cranberries

1 tablespoon tarragon vinegar or white wine vinegar

1 teaspoon lemon juice

MAKES ABOUT 7½ CUPS

DIRECTIONS

1 In a large saucepan over high heat, combine the rice and 3 cups water and bring to a boil. Stir in the lentils and cook, stirring occasionally, for 3 minutes. Reduce the heat, cover, and simmer for 15 minutes. Stir in the green beans, tomatoes, cinnamon, oregano, and a pinch of salt. Cover and simmer, stirring occasionally, until the mixture is tender, about 10 minutes.

2 Stir in the cranberries, vinegar, and lemon juice. Season to taste with salt and serve warm. Store in an airtight container in the refrigerator for up to 2 days, or freeze for up to 3 months.

SHAZI'S TIP

I use brown lentils for this recipe, but any of your favorite varieties will work well here. When combined with green beans, lentils help your little one receive a complete protein source. I sometimes swap out the beans depending on what I have on hand. Snow peas or another green legume offer the same great nutritional benefits.

CEREAL-CRUSTED FISH FINGERS

These kid-friendly, crunchy fish sticks are a sure-to-please homemade alternative to the store-bought variety. Cod is a lean white fish that is high in protein and B vitamins like niacin, folate, and vitamin B12. B vitamins are needed for energy production, with folate and vitamin B12 also helping to ensure healthy red blood cells.

INGREDIENTS

½ lb skinless cod fillet

¼ cup all-purpose flour

2 large eggs

Pinch each of salt and pepper

1½ cups corn flakes cereal, crushed

½ cup dried shredded unsweetened coconut

Green pea dipping sauce (optional; see Note)

MAKES ABOUT 8 PIECES

 NOTE

Make a green pea sauce for dipping by pureeing 1 package (10 oz) defrosted frozen green peas in a food processor until smooth.

DIRECTIONS

1 Preheat the oven to 400°F. Lightly grease a baking sheet or line with parchment paper. Cut the cod into 8 pieces, each about 4 inches long, 1 inch wide, and ½ inch thick.

2 Put the flour in a shallow dish. In a second shallow dish, beat the eggs with the salt and pepper. In a third shallow dish, mix together the corn flakes and coconut.

3 Working with one piece of fish at a time, coat on all sides with flour, shaking off any excess; then dip in the egg and turn to coat, allowing the excess to drip off; and finally coat on all sides with the corn flake–coconut mixture, pressing gently to help it adhere. Place on the prepared baking sheet and repeat with the remaining fish.

4 Bake the fish fingers, turning once halfway through baking, until they are golden brown and flake easily with a fork, 10–12 minutes total. Serve warm with the dipping sauce, if you like.

SWITCH IT UP

- *Make it gluten-free: Substitute brown rice cereal for the corn flakes and brown rice flour for the all-purpose flour.*
- *Make it egg-free: Swap out the eggs for ½ cup of regular, soy, or almond milk.*

EGG-FREE GLUTEN-FREE NUT-FREE DAIRY-FREE

QUINOA WITH CHICKEN & MIXED VEGGIES

Quinoa, an age-old gluten-free seed known as a pseudocereal, is filled with protein. This simple mix of quinoa, vegetables, and chickpeas also includes folate. With bursts of sweetness from the raisins and mint, this dish is sure to be a family favorite!

INGREDIENTS

½ lb boneless, skinless chicken breast

Salt and pepper

1 cup cooked quinoa

1 large carrot, peeled and shredded (about ½ cup)

½ cup diced red bell pepper

½ cup frozen peas, defrosted

½ cup canned chickpeas, rinsed and drained

¼ cup raisins

¼ cup chopped fresh mint leaves

2 tablespoons olive oil

Juice of 1 lemon

MAKES 8 CUPS

DIRECTIONS

1 Preheat the oven to 375°F. Lightly grease a small baking dish. Place the chicken breast in the prepared baking dish and season with salt and pepper. Cover the dish with aluminum foil and bake the chicken until opaque throughout or until an instant-read thermometer inserted into the thickest part of the breast registers 165°F, about 30 minutes. Set aside until cool enough to handle, then shred into pieces. Transfer to a bowl.

2 Add the quinoa, carrot, bell pepper, peas, chickpeas, raisins, and mint to the bowl. Toss until well mixed. Stir in the olive oil and lemon juice. Season to taste with salt and pepper. Serve at room temperature. Store leftovers in an airtight container in the refrigerator for up to 3 days, or freeze for up to 3 months.

SHAZI'S TIP

Quinoa is a dietary staple in our house particularly as it is gluten-free. If it is your first time cooking quinoa, don't be worried by the thread-like germ separating from the seed. It is totally normal.

Quinoa IS AN ANCIENT SEED HIGH IN *protein, fiber,* AND *iron.*

EGG-FREE GLUTEN-FREE NUT-FREE DAIRY-FREE

LAMB & BUTTERNUT SQUASH STEW

The collective nature of stew often makes for a well-rounded and nutritious meal. In this meaty one-pot dish, lamb contributes protein and iron—both important for body tissues. The tomatoes contain vitamin C, which boosts the absorption of iron from the spinach. The beta-carotene in the butternut squash and other vegetables is readily converted into vitamin A, which is beneficial for your little one's skin, eyes, and immune function.

INGREDIENTS

2 tablespoons vegetable oil

½ yellow onion, diced

1 lb lamb stew meat

1 can (14.5 oz) crushed tomatoes

1 small butternut squash, peeled, seeded, and cut into 1-inch cubes (about 2 cups)

1½ teaspoons finely chopped fresh rosemary

3 cups beef broth or water

1 lb frozen spinach, defrosted and squeezed dry

Salt and pepper

MAKES ABOUT 6 CUPS

DIRECTIONS

1 In a large pot over low heat, warm the vegetable oil. Add the onion and cook, stirring continuously, until softened and translucent, about 3 minutes. Add the lamb, raise the heat to medium, and cook, stirring occasionally, until heated through, about 8 minutes. Add the tomatoes and cook, stirring occasionally, for 5 minutes. Stir in the butternut squash, rosemary, and broth and bring to a boil over high heat. Reduce the heat to medium-low, cover, and simmer until the squash is tender, about 20 minutes.

2 Add the spinach to the stew and stir until blended. Cook, uncovered, until heated through, about 3 minutes. Season to taste with salt and pepper and serve warm. Store in an airtight container in the refrigerator for up to 5 days, or freeze for up to 3 months.

SWITCH IT UP

- *Spoon this savory stew over cooked brown rice, quinoa, or couscous.*

EGG-FREE GLUTEN-FREE NUT-FREE DAIRY-FREE

BEEF & SWEET POTATO STEW

Warm and hearty comfort food like this beef stew makes a great meal to enjoy not just with your toddler, but with the whole family. Incorporating chickpeas into the stew is an economical and tasty way to add fiber, protein, and micronutrients. This dish is also high in phosphorus, a mineral that supports strong bones and teeth.

INGREDIENTS

2 tablespoons vegetable oil

1 lb beef chuck roast, cut into 1-inch cubes

2–3 sweet potatoes (about 12 oz), peeled and cut into ½-inch cubes (about 3 cups)

Salt and pepper

1 can (15 oz) chickpeas, rinsed and drained

1 can (14.5 oz) crushed tomatoes

⅛ teaspoon ground cinnamon

Pinch of ground nutmeg

Pinch of ground cloves

MAKES ABOUT 6 CUPS

SHAZI'S TIP

In the colder months I look forward to the return of stews to our weekly repertoire. We enjoy a good stew or soup as a family meal on winter weekends after a long walk with our dog, Willy. It warms us up from the inside out and keeps us satisfied for hours.

DIRECTIONS

1 In a large pot over medium heat, warm the vegetable oil. Add the beef, sweet potatoes, and a pinch each of salt and pepper. Cook, stirring occasionally, for 10 minutes. Stir in the chickpeas, tomatoes, cinnamon, nutmeg, and cloves. Bring to a boil over high heat, then boil for 1 minute. Reduce the heat to low, cover, and simmer until the sweet potatoes are soft and the beef is tender, about 40 minutes.

2 Season to taste with salt and pepper and serve warm. Store in an airtight container in the refrigerator for up to 5 days, or freeze for up to 3 months.

SWITCH IT UP

- *This hearty stew is best served over cooked noodles, brown rice, or other grains.*

Farro IS AN *ancient grain* WITH A SLIGHTLY CHEWY texture.

VEGETARIAN

EGG-FREE

NUT-FREE

THREE-BEAN FARRO RISOTTO WITH LEMON & PARMESAN CHEESE

Loaded with iron, protein, and fiber, this dish is an excellent choice for a growing child. Beans and farro include iron, which is needed for healthy brain development and the formation of healthy red blood cells. Beans (three varieties are used here) have plant-based protein and complement the farro in providing essential amino acids. The beans' fiber also makes tummies happy and offers a slow, steady supply of energy.

INGREDIENTS

⅓ cup olive oil

1 small yellow onion, chopped

2¾ cups farro

4 cups chicken or vegetable broth

1 can (15 oz) pinto beans, rinsed and drained

1 can (15 oz) red kidney beans, rinsed and drained

1 can (15 oz) cannellini beans, rinsed and drained

1 cup grated Parmesan cheese

Zest of 1 lemon

Salt and pepper

MAKES 6½ CUPS

DIRECTIONS

1   In a large saucepan over medium heat, warm the olive oil. Add the onion and cook, stirring often, until translucent, 3–5 minutes. Add the farro and cook, stirring to coat the grains with oil, for 2 minutes. Add 1 cup of the broth and bring to a simmer over medium-high heat. Reduce the heat to medium-low and simmer, stirring continuously, until the broth is absorbed, about 5 minutes. Continue to cook the risotto, adding the broth a ladleful at a time and stirring until it is absorbed, until the farro is tender, about 25 minutes. When the final cup of broth has been absorbed, reduce the heat to low and stir in the beans, cheese, and lemon zest. Cook, stirring occasionally, until heated through, 3–5 minutes. Season to taste with salt and pepper.

2   Spoon into a small bowl and serve warm. Store in an airtight container in the refrigerator for up to 2 days, or freeze for up to 2 months.

SWITCH IT UP

- *For a traditional, gluten-free version, substitute Arborio rice for the farro.*

VEGETARIAN

EGG-FREE

NUT-FREE

VEGGIE PATTIES

These veggie patties, with a hint of curry, are filled with a variety of macro- and micronutrients. The potato and bread crumbs include energy-rich carbohydrates, while the beans are high in protein. The pumpkin and spinach add a boost of vitamin A, the natural antioxidant that helps to protect against disease-causing free radicals. All in all, these patties pack quite a nutritious punch! Use gluten-free bread crumbs instead of regular, if you like.

INGREDIENTS

2 small or 1 large russet potato (about 8 oz), peeled and cut into 1-inch chunks (about 1 cup)

½ cup canned pumpkin puree

1 cup canned corn kernels, drained

1 cup canned white beans, rinsed and drained

7 oz frozen spinach, defrosted and squeezed dry (about 1 cup)

¼ cup bread crumbs

2 large eggs, lightly beaten

½ cup grated Parmesan cheese

½ teaspoon yellow curry powder (see Note)

Pinch of salt

MAKES 12 PATTIES

⚡ NOTE

Curry powders are blends of many different spices and herbs. Blends can vary in heat depending on the addition of chiles. The color—yellow, green, or red curry—depends on the combination of ingredients although coriander, cumin, and turmeric are widely used. Try a few varieties to see which ones you like best.

DIRECTIONS

1 Preheat the oven to 375°F. Lightly grease a baking sheet.

2 Bring a saucepan three-fourths full of water to a boil over high heat. Add the potatoes and cook until tender, 10–12 minutes. Drain, then transfer to a large bowl. Using a potato masher or ricer, mash the potatoes until smooth. Add the pumpkin puree, corn, beans, spinach, bread crumbs, eggs, cheese, curry powder, and salt. Mix with your hands or a wooden spoon until well blended. Form about ¼ cup of the mixture into a 4-inch patty and set it on the prepared baking sheet. Repeat with the remaining mixture to form a total of 12 patties.

3 Bake, turning once halfway through baking, until firm and dry to the touch, about 20 minutes total. Serve warm. Store in an airtight container in the refrigerator for up to 5 days, or freeze for up to 4 months.

SWITCH IT UP

- *Serve warm with a dollop of Greek yogurt, sour cream, or other dipping sauce of your choice.*

- *Make storage and reheating easy by freezing patties individually or in twos to pull out of the freezer and defrost as needed.*

VEGETARIAN   EGG-FREE   NUT-FREE

12+ months

WHOLE-WHEAT TORTILLA PIZZAS WITH SMASHED BEANS & VEGGIES

This wholesome pizza alternative is high in folate, protein, and fiber, nutrients needed for red blood cells, growth, and gut health. The whole-wheat tortilla coated with the smashed beans creates a wonderful fiber-rich base for topping with vegetables of your choice.

INGREDIENTS

1 lb canned lima beans, rinsed and drained, or defrosted frozen lima beans

1 cup canned chickpeas, rinsed and drained

2 tablespoons olive oil

1 tablespoon dried oregano

Salt

4 (8-inch) whole-wheat tortillas

2 cups shredded mozzarella cheese

3 cups raw vegetables of choice (such as diced bell peppers, baby spinach leaves, and sliced mushrooms)

¼ cup chopped fresh basil leaves

MAKES 4 (8-INCH) PIZZAS

DIRECTIONS

1   Preheat the oven to 375°F. Lightly grease a baking sheet.

2   In a food processor, combine the lima beans, chickpeas, olive oil, and oregano. Puree until smooth. Season to taste with salt.

3   Spread an even layer of the bean mixture on each tortilla, dividing it equally. Place the tortillas on the prepared baking sheet. Top each tortilla with ½ cup mozzarella cheese and ¾ cup vegetables.

4   Bake the pizzas until the cheese is melted and the tortilla edges begin to crisp, 8–10 minutes. Just before serving, sprinkle each pizza with 1 tablespoon basil.

SWITCH IT UP

- *For gluten-free pizzas, use gluten-free tortillas or corn tortillas.*

- *For dairy-free pizzas, use soy cheese instead of cow's milk mozzarella.*

VEGETARIAN　　EGG-FREE　　NUT-FREE　　DAIRY-FREE

SOBA NOODLES WITH SUNFLOWER SEED BUTTER

This super-simple soba noodle dish is a wholesome meal that's quick to prepare. The sunflower butter provides a variety of nutrients, including protein, healthful fats, and vitamin E. Vitamin E is a natural antioxidant, protecting the body from harmful free radicals that can cause damage to cells. The bell peppers are a great source of vitamins A, C, and E—helping to keep kids in good health. This recipe has a larger yield and is great to share with the whole family.

INGREDIENTS

4 oz soba noodles, cooked and drained (see Note)

¼ red bell pepper, cut into small strips

¼ orange bell pepper, cut into small strips

¼ yellow bell pepper, cut into small strips

¼ cup plus 2 tablespoons sunflower seed butter

1 tablespoon pure sesame oil

Salt

MAKES 3 CUPS

NOTE

Soba is Japanese for "buckwheat." Despite the name, buckwheat is gluten-free. However, if you're concerned about gluten, always double-check the ingredient list on the package since some brands add regular wheat to the noodles.

DIRECTIONS

1 In a large bowl, combine the noodles and bell pepper strips.

2 In a small saucepan over low heat, warm the sunflower seed butter and the sesame oil, stirring occasionally, until heated through. (Alternatively, combine the sunflower seed butter and sesame oil in a microwave-safe bowl and microwave at full power until heated through, 10–20 seconds.) Pour the mixture over the noodles and bell peppers and toss gently until coated. Season to taste with salt and serve warm or at room temperature. Store in an airtight container in the refrigerator for up to 5 days, or freeze for up to 2 months.

SWITCH IT UP

- *Try rice noodles instead of soba for a gluten-free version.*

Soba noodles ARE RICH IN *fiber* & *lean protein.*

EGG-FREE NUT-FREE

AVOCADO & CHICKEN WHOLE-WHEAT PIZZAS

These pita pizzas have a balance of complex carbohydrate, lean protein, and healthful fats. The lean protein in chicken aids growth and builds body tissues. Avocado contains monounsaturated fats—the "good fats" that help to keep the heart healthy and also boost the brain and nervous system.

INGREDIENTS

½ lb boneless, skinless chicken breast (see Note)

Salt and pepper

4 (6–8-inch) whole-wheat pita breads

1½ cups shredded mozzarella cheese

1 teaspoon dried basil or oregano

2 avocados, halved, pitted, and peeled

MAKES 4 SMALL PIZZAS

SHAZI'S TIP

Does your busy schedule make it challenging to cook longer or more involved recipes? Here's one of my time-saving, convenient shortcuts: buy a roasted or rotisserie chicken instead of baking chicken from scratch at home.

DIRECTIONS

1 Preheat the oven to 375°F. Lightly grease a small baking dish. Place the chicken breast in the prepared baking dish and season with salt and pepper. Cover the dish with aluminum foil and bake the chicken until opaque throughout or until an instant-read thermometer inserted into the thickest part of the breast registers 165°F, about 30 minutes. Set aside until cool enough to handle, then shred into pieces. Set aside.

2 Lightly grease a baking sheet or line with parchment paper. Place the pita breads in a single layer on the prepared baking sheet and sprinkle with the cheese and the basil, dividing the toppings equally. Bake until the cheese melts, 3–5 minutes. Let cool slightly.

3 In a small bowl, use a fork to mash the avocados until smooth. Divide the avocado equally among the pizzas, spreading it in a thin layer over the cheese. Top with the shredded chicken. Season with salt and pepper. Cut the pizzas into quarters and serve.

4

Toddler Snacks

12+ MONTHS, FUN FOODS

Our recipes are designed to help parents think of "real" food as having great potential for snacks, like pinwheels, kebabs, and smoothies made with fresh fruits and vegetables. Turn snack time into a mini-meal instead of relying on less-nutrient-dense snack foods. To avoid over-snacking, set a snack time just as you set meal times and then stick to it. We recommend at least two hours between snacks and meals so tiny tummies have enough time to work up an appetite for a healthy meal.

Strawberries ARE A vitamin C powerhouse.

VEGETARIAN

EGG-FREE

GLUTEN-FREE

NUT-FREE

DAIRY-FREE

STRAWBERRY-BEET PUDDING WITH COCONUT & CHIA

The proof is in the pudding! This deliciously sweet twist on the creamy treat combines vitamin C–packed strawberries, antioxidant-bearing beets, and fiber-loaded chia seeds. This is a pudding with bone- and immune-boosting benefits that can be enjoyed for breakfast, a snack, or dessert. The chia seeds work as a natural thickener, adding body to the mixture without the addition of cream or eggs.

INGREDIENTS

½ cup short-grain brown rice

½ can (7 oz) light unsweetened coconut milk

½ teaspoon vanilla extract

½ cup hulled and diced strawberries

½ cup cooked, peeled, and diced beets

1 tablespoon chia seeds

Maple syrup or agave syrup for serving (optional)

Unsweetened dried shredded coconut for serving (optional)

MAKES ABOUT 2½ CUPS

DIRECTIONS

1 In a saucepan over medium heat, combine the rice, coconut milk, vanilla, and ¼ cup water and bring to a boil. Reduce the heat to low, cover, and simmer until thickened, creamy, and the rice is tender, about 30 minutes. Stir in the strawberries, beets, chia seeds, and ½ cup water. Cover and cook until slightly thickened, 8–10 minutes longer. Remove the pan from the heat and let cool slightly.

2 Ladle the pudding into serving bowls. If desired, garnish with a drizzle of maple syrup and shredded coconut and serve warm. Store leftovers in an airtight container in the refrigerator for up to 2 days.

SHAZI'S TIP

Chia is probably my all-time favorite superfood. We add it to almost anything in our house—smoothies, soups, cereal, even pasta sauces. While we use it specifically in this meal, it brings an extra nutritional boost to any puree without affecting the flavor.

VEGETARIAN   EGG-FREE   GLUTEN-FREE   DAIRY-FREE

CLEMENTINE, CARROT & RAISIN LETTUCE BOATS

These fruity, sweet, and slightly savory snacks are full of flavor and fiber from carrots and raisins. Lettuce leaves are a creative container for the fruit and veggies and make this healthful snack great for little hands. These fun-filled boats that your tot can hold are also turbocharged with vitamins A and C for eye and immune health.

INGREDIENTS

½ cup unsweetened almond butter

4 large romaine lettuce leaves

2 large carrots, peeled and shredded (about 1 cup)

4 clementines, peeled and sectioned

¼ cup raisins

MAKES 4 BOATS

DIRECTIONS

1 Spread 2 tablespoons of almond butter in the center of each romaine leaf. Evenly distribute the carrots among the leaves, sprinkling the shreds over the almond butter. Divide the clementine sections among the leaves, placing them in a line on the shredded carrots.

2 Sprinkle each leaf with 1 tablespoon raisins and serve.

SWITCH IT UP

- *For those with tree-nut allergies, use sunflower seed butter in place of the almond butter.*

NOTE

This recipe takes its inspiration from "ants on a log"—the popular after-school snack of celery, peanut butter, and raisins. It uses the same flavor profile but boosts the nutritional value by incorporating carrots and clementines (and decreases the processed sugar by using unsweetened almond butter).

VEGETARIAN   EGG-FREE   GLUTEN-FREE   NUT-FREE

BERRY, BEET & KEFIR SMOOTHIE

This delicious smoothie helps "beet" off the bad bugs with its high vitamin C content and probiotics that provide beneficial bacteria for tummies. Bellies will also be full from the protein provided by the kefir.

INGREDIENTS

2 cups plain kefir

½ can (7 oz) unsalted beets, rinsed and drained

1 cup strawberries, hulled and halved

½ cup blueberries

1 tablespoon honey or agave syrup (see Note)

Cold water, as needed

Ice for serving

MAKES ABOUT 2½ CUPS

DIRECTIONS

1 In a blender, combine the kefir, beets, strawberries, blueberries, and honey. Blend until smooth and creamy. For a thinner consistency, blend in up to ¼ cup cold water.

2 Pour into cups and serve, adding a few ice cubes to each cup.

NOTE

Agave syrup is quite popular as a natural sweetener, and rightly so. It is extracted from the blue agave plant (similar to a cactus) and is especially great for vegans who don't eat any animal products, including honey. Agave also has a lower glycemic index than honey and regular sugar, meaning that the glucose in it is released more slowly into the body postmeal, avoiding any sudden drops in energy.

VEGETARIAN EGG-FREE GLUTEN-FREE DAIRY-FREE

SUNFLOWER SEED BUTTER SMOOTHIE WITH ALMOND MILK

This creamy smoothie is a blend of powerful plant protein, potassium, and vitamins C and B6. Almond milk and sunflower seed butter include magnesium, which, along with the potassium, contributes to healthy nerve function. Dates are great for tiny tummies.

INGREDIENTS

2 cups unsweetened almond milk (see Note) or other milk

5 pitted dates, chopped (about ¼ cup)

1 ripe banana, peeled

¼ cup sunflower seed butter

Ice for serving (optional)

MAKES ABOUT 2 ½ CUPS

DIRECTIONS

1 In a blender, combine the milk, dates, banana, and sunflower seed butter. Blend until smooth and creamy.

2 Pour into cups and serve, adding a few ice cubes to each cup, if desired.

NOTE

Almonds are tree nuts (as are coconuts, pecans, pine nuts, pistachios, and walnuts). If you have a tree-nut allergy in the family, try substituting 2% or skim milk for the almond milk.

VEGETARIAN

EGG-FREE

NUT-FREE

DAIRY-FREE

SUNFLOWER SEED BUTTER, BANANA, FLAXSEED & MAPLE WRAPS

Fold an array of nutrients into this sweet twist on quesadillas. This snack is nutrient-dense and filled with vitamin B6, manganese, and vitamin C. Bananas include potassium, which is needed for a healthy heart, bones, muscles, and nerves. Flaxseeds help your child receive omega-3 (ALA) fatty acids, healthful fats that help build cells and regulate the nervous system.

INGREDIENTS

2 whole-wheat tortillas

¼ cup sunflower seed butter (see Note)

2 ripe bananas, peeled and sliced

1 tablespoon ground flaxseeds

1 tablespoon maple syrup

MAKES 2 WRAPS

 NOTE

Sunflower seed butter is a good alternative if nut allergies are a concern. In addition, it provides protein, vitamin E, fiber, zinc, and iron.

DIRECTIONS

1 Place the tortillas on a clean, flat surface. Spread 2 tablespoons sunflower seed butter over one-half of each tortilla. Place half of the banana slices in an even layer on top of the seed butter. Sprinkle each with half of the flaxseeds and drizzle with half of the maple syrup. Fold the bare side of each tortilla over the covered half to form half-moons.

2 In a large frying pan over medium heat, toast the filled tortillas, turning once, until they begin to puff and turn golden on both sides, about 5 minutes total. Transfer the tortillas to a cutting board and let cool slightly. Cut each tortilla into 4 triangles and serve warm.

SWITCH IT UP

- *Make these tasty wraps gluten-free by switching to gluten-free tortillas.*

Skewers MAKE SNACK TIME fun!

EGG-FREE   GLUTEN-FREE   NUT-FREE

12+
months

MIXED MELON, TURKEY & CHEESE KEBABS

Stack up the nutrients with these flavorful, fruity kebabs. Featuring melon and lean meat alternating with dairy, every nibble packs a punch. Cheddar cheese includes calcium to keep bones and teeth strong. Cut the melon and cheese into 1-inch cubes—just right for little hands.

INGREDIENTS

1 ¾-inch-thick slice of turkey deli meat, diced

½ cup (about 3 oz) cubed Cheddar cheese

½ cup diced cantaloupe

½ cup diced honeydew

½ cup diced seedless watermelon

MAKES 4 KEBABS

DIRECTIONS

1 Carefully thread the turkey, cheese, cantaloupe, honeydew, and watermelon onto 4 wooden skewers, alternating the ingredients and dividing them evenly.

2 Serve at once. Store in an airtight container in the refrigerator for up to 1 day.

SWITCH IT UP

- *For dairy-free kebabs, use firm tofu or grapes instead of cheese.*

- *For younger children, replace the skewers with coffee stir sticks or ice-pop sticks.*

VEGETARIAN EGG-FREE GLUTEN-FREE NUT-FREE DAIRY-FREE

WHITE BEAN & BASIL DIP

Blended-up beans and basil delivers a fiber- and protein-rich dip for snacking. You can serve the dip with whole-grain crackers, but pairing it with vitamin C–loaded bell peppers and tomatoes helps boost iron absorption for healthy red blood cells, growth, and brain development.

INGREDIENTS

- 1 can (15 oz) cannellini beans, rinsed and drained
- ⅓ cup firmly packed fresh basil leaves
- 3 tablespoons extra-virgin olive oil
- Pinch of salt (optional)
- Dippers (carrot and celery sticks, sliced bell peppers or cucumbers, crackers, or other dippers of your choice)

MAKES 1 CUP

DIRECTIONS

1. In a food processor, combine the beans, basil, olive oil, and salt, if using. Process until smooth and creamy.
2. Transfer to a bowl and serve with your favorite dippers. Store in an airtight container in the refrigerator for up to 2 days.

SHAZI'S TIP

Kids love to dip. I could always get Zane to eat more veggies by giving him carrot, cucumber, or celery sticks to dip into something delicious. Turn this healthy snack into a mini meal by using leftovers—such as fish sticks or chicken nuggets—as the dippers.

SPINACH & CHEESE MINI PIES

Incorporating spinach into a toddler's diet is easy with these delicious hand pies.
Spinach is high in iron and vitamin K, both important for healthy blood.
These mini savory pies are also filled with protein, vitamin A, folate, and fiber.

INGREDIENTS

2 tablespoons vegetable oil

½ yellow onion, finely chopped

1¼ cups (about 3 oz) firmly packed
spinach leaves

½ cup crumbled feta cheese

½ cup ricotta cheese

1 large egg, beaten

⅛ teaspoon ground nutmeg

Pinch of salt

2 unbaked 9-inch piecrusts

MAKES 8 MINI PIES

DIRECTIONS

1 Preheat the oven to 350°F. Lightly grease a
baking sheet.

2 In a large frying pan over medium heat, warm the
vegetable oil. Add the onion and cook, stirring
continuously, until softened and translucent,
3–5 minutes. Add the spinach and cook until
the leaves are fully wilted, about 5 minutes. Using
a slotted spoon, transfer the spinach mixture
to a bowl, reserving the liquid in the pan. Let cool.

3 Add the feta cheese, ricotta cheese, egg, nutmeg,
and salt to the cooled spinach and stir until well
combined. Cut each pie dough round into
quarters. Spoon 1½ 2 tablespoons of the spinach
filling onto one-half of one piece of pie dough.
Fold the bare half over the filling and pinch the
edges to seal well. Place the filled mini pie on the
prepared baking sheet. Repeat with the remaining
filling and pie dough pieces.

4 Bake the pies until lightly browned, about
20 minutes. Remove from the oven and serve
warm. Store in an airtight container in the
refrigerator for up to 2 days, or freeze for
up to 1 month.

VEGETARIAN

EGG-FREE

GLUTEN-FREE

NUT-FREE

TOFU, TOMATO & SWEET PEPPER KEBABS WITH CHEESE

Have fun packing in the protein with these tofu-based kebabs. In addition to being low in fat and high in protein, tofu includes isoflavones, which act as natural antioxidants, and alpha-linolenic acid, the essential omega-3 fatty acid that helps protect against disease and supports brain health. One kebab is the perfect size for a super snack.

INGREDIENTS

7 oz extra-firm tofu, cut into 1½-inch cubes

4 oz cheese, cut into 1½-inch cubes

½ orange bell pepper, cut into 1-inch squares

½ yellow bell pepper, cut into 1-inch squares

8 grape or cherry tomatoes

8 fresh basil leaves

MAKES 4 KEBABS

DIRECTIONS

1 Carefully thread the tofu, cheese, bell peppers, tomatoes, and basil onto each of 4 skewers, alternating the ingredients and dividing them evenly.

SWITCH IT UP

- *Make the kebabs dairy-free by omitting the cheese.*

- *For younger children, replace the skewers with coffee stir sticks or ice-pop sticks.*

EVERY HUE OF *bell pepper* IS AN *awesome source* OF *vitamin C.*

BAKED APPLES WITH CHEDDAR CHEESE & PUMPKIN SEEDS

An apple a day keeps the doctor away! Apples deliver fiber and vitamin C. The sprinkle of pumpkin seeds adds a slight crunch, as well as magnesium and zinc. Zinc plays a role in immune function and wound healing.

INGREDIENTS

2 large red apples, halved and cored

2 tablespoons maple syrup, agave syrup, or brown sugar

⅛ teaspoon ground cinnamon

½ cup shredded Cheddar cheese

2 tablespoons raw pumpkin seeds

MAKES 4 APPLE HALVES

DIRECTIONS

1 Preheat the oven to 350°F. Lightly grease a 9-by-13-inch baking dish.

2 Place the apple halves, cut side up, in the prepared baking dish. Drizzle or sprinkle the sweetener over the apples, dividing it evenly, then sprinkle with the cinnamon. Top each apple half with 2 tablespoons Cheddar cheese and sprinkle with 1½ teaspoons pumpkin seeds.

3 Cover the dish with aluminum foil and bake until the apples are tender, about 35 minutes. Remove the foil and let cool, then serve. Store in an airtight container in the refrigerator for up to 2 days.

SWITCH IT UP

- *You can play with different types of cheese and fruit in this vitamin C–boosting snack. Pears make a great substitute since, like apples, they hold their shape well when baked. Also, if you choose a red-skinned variety, your little one will be getting the added benefit of beta-carotene, an anti-inflammatory antioxidant.*

VEGETARIAN

EGG-FREE

NUT-FREE

DAIRY-FREE

SAVORY SUPER SNACK MIX

Trail mix is a super snack for kids of all ages. This combination of seeds and whole grains is filled with fiber and B vitamins, both needed for healthy digestion and carbohydrate metabolism. The sunflower seeds are high in vitamin E, a fat-soluble vitamin beneficial to healthy immune function.

INGREDIENTS

2 cups whole-grain cereal, such as whole-wheat O-shaped cereal or gluten-free cereal

2 cups popped popcorn

1 cup pretzel nuggets, mini pretzels, or pretzel sticks

1 cup dehydrated snap peas or green beans, or vegetable chips

3 tablespoons semisweet chocolate chips

2 tablespoons toasted pumpkin seeds

MAKES ABOUT 6 CUPS

DIRECTIONS

1 In a large bowl, mix the cereal, popcorn, pretzels, snap peas, chocolate chips, and pumpkin seeds.

2 Serve immediately, or store in an airtight container at cool room temperature for up to 3 days.

VEGETARIAN

EGG-FREE

NUT-FREE

DAIRY-FREE

SWEET SUPER SNACK MIX

This combo adds in the sweet without contributing a lot of refined sugar to the mix. The sweetness comes from the natural sugars that reside in dried fruits—in this case, apples, bananas, and raisins. Combined with the seeds and whole grains, the mixture helps your toddler receive fiber and B vitamins, both needed to keep tummies happy.

INGREDIENTS

2½ cups whole-grain cereal, such as whole-wheat O-shaped cereal or gluten-free cereal

1½ cups dried apple rings

1 cup dried banana chips

½ cup beet chips

¼ cup raisins

¼ cup sunflower seeds

MAKES ABOUT 6 CUPS

DIRECTIONS

1 In a large bowl, mix the cereal, apple rings, banana chips, beet chips, raisins, and sunflower seeds.

2 Serve immediately, or store in an airtight container at cool room temperature for up to 3 days.

SHAZI'S TIP

These nut-free trail mixes are perfect on-the-go snacks. I often carry a bag of the savory version with me when we go out with Zane, and it has been a lifesaver when hunger hits. Making these recipes gluten-free is easy; most major grocery stores now carry gluten-free cereals and pretzels in the natural products section.

VEGETARIAN

NUT-FREE

PUMPKIN & ZUCCHINI MUFFINS

Zucchini bread just got better! The combination of pumpkin, pumpkin seeds, and zucchini provides a serving of fiber while also enriching these muffins in vitamin A, potassium, and protein. Applesauce added to the batter keeps the muffins nice and moist.

INGREDIENTS

1½ cups whole-wheat flour

½ cup all-purpose flour

1 teaspoon baking soda

1 teaspoon baking powder

1 large zucchini, shredded (about 1 cup)

1 cup canned pumpkin puree

3 large eggs, lightly beaten

⅓ cup plain Greek yogurt

⅓ cup applesauce

⅓ cup agave syrup

⅓ cup raw pumpkin seeds

MAKES 16 MUFFINS

DIRECTIONS

1 Preheat the oven to 375°F. Lightly grease 16 cups of 2 standard muffin pans or line with paper liners.

2 In a bowl, mix the flours, baking soda, and baking powder. In a large bowl, stir together the zucchini, pumpkin puree, eggs, yogurt, applesauce, and agave syrup. Gradually stir the flour mixture into the zucchini mixture, stirring until combined.

3 Evenly divide the batter among the prepared muffin cups, scooping about ¼ cup batter into each cup. Sprinkle evenly with the pumpkin seeds. Bake until a toothpick inserted into the centers comes out clean, 18–20 minutes.

4 Remove the pan from the oven and place on a cooling rack. Let the muffins cool in the pan for 10 minutes, then remove from the pan and let cool completely. Store in an airtight container at room temperature for up to 3 days, or freeze for up to 3 months.

SWITCH IT UP

- *Don't be afraid to adapt the recipe to your liking. Exchange the pumpkin seeds with sliced almonds or pecans, if you like. Or swap out the pumpkin seeds in favor of dried cranberries or dried blueberries for spunky flavor and natural antioxidants.*

Pumpkin's vitamin A
IS GOOD FOR *eyesight*.

Small vegetables LIKE CHERRY TOMATOES ARE great for stuffing.

VEGETARIAN

EGG-FREE

NUT-FREE

MINI VEGETABLES STUFFED WITH YOGURT, FARRO & RAISINS

Stuffed vegetable bites are fun for little fingers, and they're a wonderfully balanced snack with complex carbohydrate, protein, calcium, phosphorus, vitamin C, and more, depending on your choice of vegetable. And the addition of yogurt mixes in even more protein and calcium—always good for growing bodies!

INGREDIENTS

1 pint cherry tomatoes, 24 baby bell peppers, or 2 English cucumbers

1 cup cooked and cooled whole-grain farro

½ cup plain Greek yogurt

¼ cup raisins

¼ cup chopped unsulfured dried apricots

¼ teaspoon dried dill

¼ teaspoon dried oregano

MAKES ABOUT 2 DOZEN SNACKS

DIRECTIONS

1 Use a melon baller or baby spoon to hollow out the vegetables. If using cherry tomatoes or baby bell peppers, cut off the tops and carefully scoop out the interiors. If using cucumbers, cut each one crosswise into 1½-inch pieces and carefully scoop out the center portion, leaving the bottom to form a cup.

2 In a bowl, mix the farro, yogurt, raisins, apricots, dill, and oregano. Spoon the mixture into the vegetables and serve. Store in an airtight container in the refrigerator for up to 3 days.

SWITCH IT UP

- *This dried fruit and grain mixture also makes a great filling for mushroom caps and celery, or a topping for crackers or a thin slice of whole-wheat bread.*

VEGETARIAN

EGG-FREE

DAIRY-FREE

NO-BAKE CRANBERRY & OAT GRANOLA BITES

Soft and chewy granola bites are sure to be a go-to snack favorite. They are great to have on hand for a quick, fiber-rich nibble that satisfies a sweet craving. Cranberries help to keep the kidneys healthy and also include flavonoids to protect against disease.

INGREDIENTS

1½ cups old-fashioned rolled oats

1 cup unsweetened dried cranberries

¼ cup ground flaxseeds

¼ cup honey

¼ cup maple syrup

½ cup unsweetened almond butter

MAKES 40-50 BITES

DIRECTIONS

1 Line a baking sheet with parchment paper.

2 In a bowl, stir together the oats, cranberries, flaxseeds, honey, and maple syrup.

3 In a small saucepan over medium heat, warm the almond butter until melted. (Alternatively, microwave the almond butter in a microwave-safe bowl at full power, stirring once or twice, until melted, about 30 seconds.) Pour the almond butter over the oat mixture and stir until evenly combined.

4 Using your hands, scoop up 1 tablespoon of the oat mixture, roll it between your palms to form a ball, and place it on the prepared baking sheet. Repeat with the remaining oat mixture. Cover the balls lightly with wax paper or aluminum foil and refrigerate until firm, 1–3 hours. Serve at once, store in an airtight container in the refrigerator for up to 2 days, or freeze for up to 1 month.

VEGETARIAN

NUT-FREE

BRAN MUFFINS WITH DRIED APRICOTS

Bran is filled with insoluble fiber, which keeps your baby's tummy happy. Dotted with dried apricots, these bran muffins contain pockets of tender sweetness while also helping your toddler receive the iron needed for good health and development.

INGREDIENTS

- ¾ cup bran flakes cereal
- 1¼ cups milk
- 1½ cups whole-wheat flour
- ¼ cup sugar
- 1 teaspoon baking soda
- 1 teaspoon baking powder
- 2 large eggs, lightly beaten
- ¼ cup vegetable oil
- 1 cup chopped dried apricots

MAKES 15 MUFFINS

DIRECTIONS

1 Preheat the oven to 350°F. Lightly grease 15 cups of 2 standard muffin pans or line with paper liners.

2 In a large bowl, combine the bran flakes and milk and set aside for 3–5 minutes to allow the cereal to absorb the milk. In a bowl, whisk together the flour, sugar, baking soda, and baking powder.

3 When the bran flakes have fully absorbed the milk, gently stir with a fork to break up the flakes. Add the eggs and oil and stir until combined. Using a wooden spoon, gradually stir in the flour mixture until blended. Gently fold in the dried apricots.

4 Evenly divide the batter among the prepared muffin cups. Bake until a toothpick inserted into the centers comes out clean, 18–20 minutes.

5 Remove the pan from the oven and place on a cooling rack. Let the muffins cool in the pan for 10 minutes, then remove from the pan and let cool completely. Store in an airtight container at room temperature for up to 3 days, or freeze for up to 3 months.

SWITCH IT UP

- *Don't let allergies restrict your toddler from this delicious recipe! If your little guy has dairy allergies, substitute the regular milk with soy, coconut, hemp, or rice milk.*

VEGETARIAN

 EGG-FREE

 GLUTEN-FREE

 NUT-FREE

DAIRY-FREE

AVOCADO, HONEYDEW & MINT SMOOTHIE

Whip up this simple three-ingredient smoothie in a flash to make a fresh and frothy snack. It's rich in vitamin C and natural sugars to provide the right boost of energy for those active toddlers. They will love the creamy consistency and natural sweetness!

INGREDIENTS

2 cups cubed honeydew

½ avocado, pitted and peeled

2 tablespoons fresh mint leaves

Cold water, as needed

Ice for serving (optional)

MAKES ABOUT 2½ CUPS

DIRECTIONS

1 In a blender, combine the honeydew, avocado, and mint. Blend until smooth and creamy. For a thinner consistency, blend in up to ¼ cup cold water.

2 Pour into cups and serve, adding a few ice cubes to each cup, if desired.

 NOTE

Save the pit from the avocado for a planting activity with the kids! Simply insert four evenly spaced toothpicks into the pit and set atop a glass of water, allowing the bottom of the pit to become submerged. Find a nice sunny spot for the glass, and wait for the first signs of your avocado "tree." Look for a sprout in about six weeks.

Honeydew melon
IS A GOOD SOURCE OF
vitamin B6, folate,
AND potassium.

VEGETARIAN

NUT-FREE

CHOCOLATE CHIP, BANANA & QUINOA MUFFINS

These sweet muffins are low in sugar, low in fat, and simply scrumptious as breakfast, a snack, or dessert! They're mighty nutritious—loaded with vitamin B6, manganese, vitamin C, and potassium. Manganese is a trace mineral that helps the body to use carbohydrate and fat and also plays a role in tissue regeneration.

INGREDIENTS

1 cup all-purpose flour

½ cup cooked quinoa

⅓ cup sugar

1 teaspoon baking soda

1 teaspoon baking powder

1 ripe banana, peeled and mashed

2 large eggs, lightly beaten

¼ cup milk

¼ cup applesauce

¼ cup canola oil

1 teaspoon vanilla extract

1 cup semisweet chocolate chips

MAKES 15 MUFFINS

DIRECTIONS

1 Preheat the oven to 350°F. Lightly grease 15 cups of 2 standard muffin pans or line with paper liners.

2 In a bowl, stir together the flour, quinoa, sugar, baking soda, and baking powder. In a large bowl, whisk together the banana, eggs, milk, applesauce, oil, and vanilla. Gradually add the flour mixture to the banana mixture, stirring until combined. Gently fold in the chocolate chips.

3 Evenly divide the batter among the prepared muffin cups. Bake until a toothpick inserted into the centers comes out clean, 18–20 minutes.

4 Remove the pan from the oven and place on a cooling rack. Let the muffins cool in the pan for 10 minutes, then remove from the pan and let cool completely. Store in an airtight container at room temperature for up to 3 days, or freeze for up to 3 months.

SWITCH IT UP

- *For a gluten-free variation of this muffin, simply use gluten-free flour in place of the all-purpose flour.*

TAHINI, BANANA & CACAO DIP

This tasty snack is a great dip for crackers, pretzels, or sliced apples. It's not too salty and not too sweet. The bananas provide potassium and vitamin C, while the milk adds protein. The dark cacao also includes flavonoids—antioxidants thought to be beneficial for heart health.

INGREDIENTS

- 1½ cups milk
- ¼ cup tahini
- ¼ cup cacao nibs
- 1 ripe banana, peeled and sliced
- ¼ teaspoon ground cinnamon
- ¼ teaspoon vanilla extract
- Dippers (crackers, pretzels, sliced apples, or other dippers of your choice)

MAKES ABOUT 2½ CUPS

DIRECTIONS

1. In a food processor, combine the milk, tahini, cacao nibs, banana, cinnamon, and vanilla. Pulse until the mixture is smooth.

2. Place ½ cup of the dip into a bowl and serve with your favorite dippers. Store in an airtight container in the refrigerator for up to 2 days.

BERRIES, *especially blueberries,* ARE A *superfood* LOADED WITH ANTIOXIDANTS

GRILLED NUT BUTTER & BERRY SANDWICHES WITH CHIA

These tasty grilled sandwiches include the nutrients that can benefit gut, heart, and immune health. Fresh berries and chia seeds include more fiber, magnesium, and protein than the classic peanut butter and jelly sandwich. Chia seeds have fiber, protein, and omega-3 (ALA) fatty acids, as well as iron, calcium, magnesium, and zinc.

INGREDIENTS

½ cup hulled and diced strawberries

½ cup blueberries

½ cup halved raspberries

2 tablespoons chia seeds

4 slices whole-wheat bread

¼ cup nut butter of choice

1 cup vanilla Greek yogurt

MAKES 2 SANDWICHES

SHAZI'S TIP

When we started thinking about the Enlightened Nutrition Philosophy for our recipes, we wanted to add as many nutrients as we could from nature's most powerful food sources. Chia is particularly amazing. Chia seeds are naturally gluten-free and contain very high concentrations of omega-3s (ALA), fiber, minerals, and vitamins.

DIRECTIONS

1 In a bowl, combine the strawberries, blueberries, raspberries, and chia seeds. Using the back of a wooden spoon or a potato masher, mash the berries until they are juicy and well combined.

2 Lay out the bread slices on a clean, flat surface. Divide the berry mixture between 2 of the slices and spread to cover the entire surface. Spread half of the nut butter onto each of the remaining 2 bread slices. Invert the slices onto the berry-covered slices to form 2 sandwiches.

3 Lightly spray a large frying pan with nonstick cooking spray and place over medium heat. Toast the sandwiches, turning once, until golden brown on both sides, about 6 minutes total. Transfer the sandwiches to a cutting board and let cool slightly.

4 Cut each sandwich into quarters and serve with the vanilla yogurt for dipping.

SWITCH IT UP

- *Frozen berries work just as well as fresh berries in this recipe.*

VEGETARIAN

EGG-FREE

NUT-FREE

CREAM CHEESE PINWHEELS WITH BELL PEPPERS

Roll up the nutrients in these fun pinwheels that are perfect for hungry little tots. The peppers add fun pops of color and are a great source of vitamin C. The cream cheese has protein and calcium. Calcium is good for bones, while protein and vitamin C work together in the body to build connective tissue.

INGREDIENTS

¾ cup whipped cream cheese

⅓ orange bell pepper, finely diced (about ⅓ cup)

⅓ red bell pepper, finely diced (about ⅓ cup)

⅓ yellow bell pepper, finely diced (about ⅓ cup)

1 teaspoon dried dill

4 whole-wheat tortillas

MAKES 24 PINWHEELS

DIRECTIONS

1 In a bowl, combine the cream cheese, bell peppers, and dill. Stir with a rubber spatula until well mixed.

2 Lay out the tortillas on a clean, flat surface. Evenly divide the cream cheese mixture among the tortillas, using about 3 tablespoons per tortilla. Using the spatula, spread to completely cover the surface. Tightly roll each tortilla into a log. Using a serrated knife, slice each log into 6 pieces and serve. Store in an airtight container in the refrigerator for up to 2 days, or freeze for up to 2 months.

SWITCH IT UP

- *Dairy allergy? Adapt this fun snack using delicious dairy-free options! Some tasty alternatives include tofu cream cheese, soy cream cheese, or hummus.*

- *Make the spirals gluten-free by substituting gluten-free tortillas for whole-wheat ones.*

THESE **colorful pinwheels** BRING
THE PERFECT BALANCE OF **crunchy**
AND **creamy** TO snack time.

INDEX

ACKNOWLEDGMENTS

This cookbook would not have been possible without the hard work from many members of our Happy Family and The Creative Kitchen teams. We especially want to thank Nicole Auker, Amy Marlow, Rebecca Kovalcik, Regina Fechter, Helen Bernstein, Marykate Maher, Jess Sarte, Anne Laraway, Grace Maniscalco, Katie Auerbach, Marcu Alexander, and Pete Soyer. Your generous cooking tips and beautiful designs have made this book come alive!

Weldon Owen wishes to thank the following people for their generous support in producing this book: Eduardo Barrera, Lesley Bruynesteyn, Conor Buckley, Chelsie Craig, Ken DellaPenta, Gloria Geller, Rachel Markowitz, Jessica O'Brien, Tamara White, and Dawn Yanagihara.

weldon**owen**

Weldon Owen is a division of Bonnier Publishing
1045 Sansome Street, Suite 100, San Francisco, CA 94111
www.weldonowen.com

The Happy Family Organic Superfoods Cookbook
A WELDON OWEN PRODUCTION
Copyright © 2016 Weldon Owen, Inc.

Printed and bound in China

First printed in 2016
10 9 8 7 6 5 4 3 2 1

Library of Congress Cataloging-in-Publication data is available.

ISBN 13: 978-1-68188-049-5
ISBN 10: 1-68188-049-0

WELDON OWEN, INC
President & Publisher Roger Shaw
SVP, Sales & Marketing Amy Kaneko
Finance & Operations Director Philip Paulick

Associate Publisher Amy Marr
Senior Editor Lisa Atwood

Creative Director Kelly Booth
Senior Production Designer Rachel Lopez Metzger

Production Director Chris Hemesath
Associate Production Director Michelle Duggan

Imaging Manager Don Hill

Photographer Tara Donne
Food Stylist María del Mar Cuadra
Prop Stylist Martha Bernabe

Additional Photography: Kana Okada: page 2, top right and bottom left; Alexandra Grablewski/Getty Images: page 18; Catherine Delahaye/Getty Images: page 30; Shutterstock: page 64; Happy Family: page 98